D0792132

GREAT COLLEGE FOOTBALL COACHES

GREAT COLLEGE FOOTBALL COACHES

JACK CLARY

GALLERY BOOKS
An imprint of W.H. Smith Publishers Inc.
112 Madison Avenue
New York, New York 10016

Published by Gallery Books
A Division of W H Smith Publishers Inc.
112 Madison Avenue
New York, New York 10016

Produced by
Brompton Books Corp.
15 Sherwood Place
Greenwich, CT 06830

Copyright © 1990 Brompton Books Corp.

All rights reserved. No part of this
book may be reproduced or transmitted
in any form or by any means without written
permission from the copyright owner.

ISBN 0-8317-3986-X

Printed in Hong Kong

10 9 8 7 6 5 4 3 2

This book is dedicated to all the men who
have stood on the sidelines on Saturday
afternoons and poured their spirit into
making college football a national treasure.

Page 1: *Michigan's Bo
Schembechler retired
after the 1989 season
as the fifth winningest
coach in Division 1-A
history, with 234
victories. He took his
Michigan teams to 17
bowl games in 21
seasons, had 13 Big
Ten titles or co-
championships, and
finished with an .838
conference winning
percentage.*

Page 2: *Woody Hayes
of Ohio State places
fourth on the all-time
winningest Division
1-A coach roster, with
238 wins. His
Buckeye teams won or
shared 13 Big Ten
titles, and three of
them were national
champions.*

Below: *Alabama
coach Bear Bryant
enjoys the jubilation of
his 314th career win
on November 14, 1981,
matching Amos
Alonzo Stagg's record.
By the time he had
retired after the 1982
season, he was the all-
time winningest
Division 1-A coach,
with 323 victories,
including 24
consecutive winning
seasons, 13 SEC
titles, six national
championships and 23
consecutive bowl
appearances.*

TABLE OF CONTENTS

INTRODUCTION

The game of college football may have started as an amalgam of English soccer and rugby, but it has evolved into a distinctly American pastime that can make a crisp, sunny fall Saturday afternoon a special occasion. For those who love the game, there is nothing like those Saturdays, from the cozy warmth of early September, with the blazing colors of autumn providing an artist's backdrop, to the chill winds of late November, when bundling up (and snuggling) becomes a necessity in most parts of the country.

We honor the game's stars who we come to watch on these fall afternoons: quarterbacks who can throw long and short with deadly accuracy;

Right: *Paul (Bear) Bryant is the all-time winningest coach in Division 1-A football, with 323 victories.*

Far right: *Woody Hayes of Ohio State won more games than any other Big Ten coach in history.*

Right: *Entering the 1990s, no other active Division 1-A coach has won more games than Joe Paterno of Penn State.*

Far right: *Bo Schembechler of Michigan retired after the 1989 season as Michigan's most successful football coach.*

backs who can dance, spin, leap, catch and move with power and speed, and with a dancer's grace and style; receivers whose hands may be soft as velvet but which are capable of absorbing footballs as a sponge absorbs water; and wonderfully skilled linemen who have the athleticism to combine hundreds of pounds of weight and strength, and yet still perform feats of great force with equal parts of skill and dexterity.

But every Saturday, a group of men brings this panoply into focus, men who are to football teams what great conductors are to symphony orchestras. They are the coaches, and this book honors 40 who have made a great impact on the game of football during the past century.

However, before anyone can fully appreciate what these men have achieved, it also is necessary to focus on precisely what a coach is – and is not – because too often we slough off their work with a "hired to be fired" attitude that shows a complete disdain for their special skills. It is the American way that everyone who watches a football game, from the oldest grad to the rawest freshman, is a coach unto himself and thinks he has the answer to every problem. When the answers of the grandstand coaches don't fit with those offered by the men who must make the real decisions, then often there is scorn and derision, always there is impatience and rarely is their compliance, even in victory. Every coach in this book, regardless of his success, has experienced, or is experiencing, these reactions.

To the contrary, football coaches should be an honored segment of our higher-educational communities. They are teachers in every sense of the word, doing on the gridiron during practice sessions what others on their school's faculties are doing in lecture halls and classrooms. Their subject is the game of football, with all of its mind-bending peculiarities and tactical intricacies, yet with at least as much emphasis on mental discipline and application to learning as is demanded by mathematicians, scientists, and purveyors of the classics.

Their classrooms are not air-conditioned in the heat, nor heated in the cold, but they are outdoors on grass fields, often scarred into muddy gulches by the constant work of young men drilling and learning their skills to entertain thousands each Saturday afternoon, and bring a measure of glory to their school. How well the coaches do their job is there for all to see each week, not once a semester, nor once a year, nor hidden under the guise of endless research. The results are dependent upon the ever-changing minds and bodies of young men who must perform under great mental and physical pressures.

This book celebrates only some of the coaches who have excelled in all the skills which a coach must possess – and it pointedly omits those such as

Left: *Eddie Robinson of Grambling has won more games than any coach in football history, and is entering his sixth decade of coaching at Grambling University.*

Left: *John McKay popularized the "student body right and left" offense at USC with his great running backs Mike Garrett and O.J. Simpson, both of whom won the Heisman Trophy.*

Barry Switzer, Danny Ford and Jackie Sherrill, who were successful on the field, but whose approach to the game and apparent disinterest in the rules which govern it have dishonored their efforts.

Like any book that must select a limited number of achievers in a given subject, this book obviously will omit candidates who others will favor. But the means of selection was based not only on the number of lifetime victories, but on the coach's overall contribution to the game and its participants; on his

Clark Shaughnessy, Lou Little, Matty Bell, Frank Cavanaugh, Jim Tatum, Bob Blackman, Don Farout, Red Sanders; and those currently excelling, such as Don James, Johnny Majors, Bill Mallory, Bill Dooley, Grant Teaff, Jim Young, Don Nehlen, Jim Sweeney, Lavell Edwards, all of whom have won more than 130 games.

Then there are those who have been eminently successful at lower levels of intercollegiate competition, where often men devote their entire professional lives to coaching young men in what has become known as a "small college atmosphere." They have the same dedication to the principles of the game and the same drive to excel as their contemporaries working at the major levels, and the outcome of the games are no less important. Their charges are students who may not be skilled enough to play at the higher levels, but who simply love to play football and look to these men to help them satisfy that yearning: coaches such as John Gagliardi at St. John's in Minnesota and Ron Schipper at Central Iowa, and others now retired who also won more than 200 games: Darrell Mudra, Arnett Mumford, John Merritt, Fred Long.

The 40 men in this book represent those who have coached the game of college football at every level with skill, affection, and total dedication.

Right: *Fielding H. (Hurry Up) Yost built college football's first great dynasty in the game's modern era, winning 56 straight games in his first five seasons at Michigan (1901-05).*

Below: *Amos Alonzo Stagg is the "Father of American Football" because of his many innovations that helped the development of the sport.*

Opposite: *Knute Rockne of Notre Dame is still college football's most recognized coach, thanks to his team's exploits and his ability to popularize them.*

character as a person and a teacher; and his number of significant achievements such as national and conference championships, and his ability to make his teams consistently successful at the highest levels of intercollegiate competition.

In so stating, one cannot just walk away without also recognizing those whose exploits are not detailed, but who, for lack of space, simply could not be included: coaches who have excelled such as Warren Woodson, Bob Devaney, Frank Broyles, Carl Snavely, Shug Jordan, Percy Haughton, H. O. (Fritz) Crisler, Bob Woodruff, Ossie Solem, Dr. Henry Williams, Ray Morrison, Francis Schmidt,

DR. EDDIE ANDERSON

Record:

Loras (1922-24)	16-6-2
De Paul (1925-32)	21-22-3
Holy Cross (1933-38)	47-7-4
Iowa (1939-42)	19-14-1
(1946-49)	16-19-1
Holy Cross (1950-64)	82-60-4

Below: Dr. Eddie Anderson (left) had two coaching tours at Holy Cross. His second began in 1950 when his captain was tackle Tex Donnalley (right). He won 82 games during that second tour and 129 in all, making him the school's all-time winningest coach.

Eddie Anderson was a scrawny, scared freshman from Mason City, Iowa, seeking a job as an end when he reported to Notre Dame's practice field in 1918. The Irish had a new head coach named Knute Rockne and though he hadn't even met this future football immortal, Anderson's knees were knocking with nervousness. Rockne glanced at him and asked:

"How much do you weigh, son?"

"One hundred and forty-nine pounds, sir, and I stand five-ten," the youth stammered.

"What position have you played?" Rockne asked him.

"End, sir."

Rockne snapped: "I have 16 right ends and 14 left ends!"

"I guess I'm a left end then, sir," Anderson replied.

Rockne chuckled because as a master of the quick comeback, he appreciated one himself, so he tossed Eddie a pair of oversized football pants.

"Those are lucky pants, son, so don't lose them," he told him. "Take them to the tailor and have them sewed and patched."

Actually the pants were the only ones left, but they did turn out to be lucky because a few weeks later, Anderson was in Cleveland for Notre Dame's opening game against Case Tech. Rockne started the second unit, but Case recovered a fumble after the kickoff and scored. So he sent the regulars into the game, and on a hunch, put Anderson in with them. Thus began a career in which Anderson played with another Irish immortal, George Gipp, and had only one losing game in four seasons, gaining All-America honors and the captaincy of Notre Dame's 1921 team in his senior year. Most importantly, his time on the gridiron led him to a football coaching career that ultimately sent him to the Hall of Fame as one of just a handful of coaches to win more than 200 games at the game's highest level.

But football was not the only important thing in Anderson's life. He diligently pursued medical studies, working his way through Rush Medical School while playing pro football with the Chicago Cardinals and coaching at DePaul University. Unlike Jock Sutherland, the great Pitt coach who received a dental degree but never saw a patient, Anderson juggled his coaching and his medical work throughout his life, but always seemed to be caring for the young, the indigent, the aging, and for a time, the war veterans. Seven years after he had retired as head coach at Holy Cross, Anderson was a senior physician at a state facility in Connecticut. "There was never a time when I thought I would drop medicine for football," he once noted.

Thankfully, he also never dropped football for medicine. Anderson helped both Holy Cross – twice – and Iowa to some of their greatest seasons. He first came to Holy Cross after receiving his medical degree in 1933 and rolled up a 47-7-4 record in the next eight seasons, including an undefeated 1935 team that was the first in the school's history. Only a 13-13 tie against Manhattan College kept it from being perfect. Two ties in 1937 spoiled a perfect season again, and a one-point loss to Carnegie Tech cost his 1938 team a perfect record.

Anderson's Holy Cross teams always sparkled on defense, his 1937 team giving up only 19 points

in 10 games. For his last three seasons, he had a marvelous offensive performer in Bill Osmanski, who made an auspicious debut as a sophomore by returning an interception 76 yards for his team's only touchdown, enabling the Crusaders to beat Dartmouth for the first time.

Anderson always considered Osmanski, and Nile Kinnick, his Heisman Trophy All-American back at Iowa, as his two best players. Osmanski, who later became a dentist and preceded Anderson as coach at Holy Cross before Eddie returned for his second stint there, was a great runner, pass receiver and defensive player. Anderson often likened his style to that of Tom Harmon, the 1940 Heisman Trophy winner at Michigan.

With players such as Ronnie Cahill, who Anderson compared to Kinnick, and Osmanski, Anderson began gaining a reputation for performing the seemingly impossible, which earned him the label "Architect of the Upset." This started in 1935 when a 33-yard field goal by Rex Kidd helped his Crusaders to a 3-0 upset victory over a Colgate team that had lost only three games in the previous three seasons.

At Iowa he really began turning miracles. Anderson longed to return to his home state, and he was offered the job in 1939 because the Hawkeyes had won only two games in the two previous seasons. The athletic department was just about as destitute as the football team, and some said that bonds sold to finance its stadium could then be purchased for ten cents on the dollar.

Anderson was aware of the enormity of his task, and that season he turned out one of the school's greatest and most heroic teams, nicknamed the "Iron Men" since many of its players did 60-minute duty. Soft-spoken at practice, but blunt and stern

Above: *Anderson's foremost rival at Holy Cross was Boston College. He won four of six games against the Eagles during his first stint as head coach, but ran into trouble in his first game as the Crusaders lost a close one, 13-9. Here Johnny Fritas of BC passes to Joe Killilea for a 10-yard gain in that 1933 game.*

Left: *Nile Kinnick won the 1939 Heisman Trophy while playing for Dr. Anderson at the University of Iowa. Anderson considered Kinnick, who was killed during World War II, one of the two best players he ever coached. The other was Bill Osmanski at Holy Cross.*

Above: *Kinnick, who was just 167 pounds, rarely was taken out of a game during his Heisman Trophy season. Here, he scores the winning touchdown when the Hawkeyes upset Notre Dame that year.*

when necessary, Anderson never shouted or berated players, and seemed most tolerant with those whose desire and determination exceeded their talent. Yet, the members of that 1939 team admitted years later that they never worked so hard at football in their lives, and one said, "It would have been awful if it hadn't paid off."

This was exactly the kind of handling those whipped players needed to restore their spirit, and it showed in the first game when Iowa defeated North Dakota 49-0, and then came from behind to upset Indiana 32-29. A 39-7 loss to Michigan in the third game and an upset tie against Northwestern in the season's final game cost Iowa the Big Ten title, but Anderson upset Notre Dame and Minnesota and, in one of the season's strangest games, got two blocked punt safeties from Mike Enich to beat Purdue 4-0. "Shucks, we didn't even need that second safety. We just wanted to make it decisive," Hawkeyes' line coach Jim Harris noted.

The players, even with their iron man stints, never forgot who was boss. At the halftime of one game, Anderson fixed one of his patented icy stares on quarterback Al Couppee, who twice had given the ball to a back other than Kinnick when Iowa was inside the 10-yard line.

"Couppee, when we get inside the ten, there is only one man we should always use," he said. "Do you know the guy?"

"Then I had to go over and shake hands with Nile," Couppee related some years later. "But (Anderson) certainly made his point for the rest of the season."

Kinnick, who weighed only 167 pounds, really was the point man for Anderson in the Hawkeyes' great season. He was a fine passer, with 11 touchdown passes that year, two in the fourth quarter to beat Minnesota, and he scored the winning touchdown against Notre Dame. He played six games without relief and was awarded the Heisman

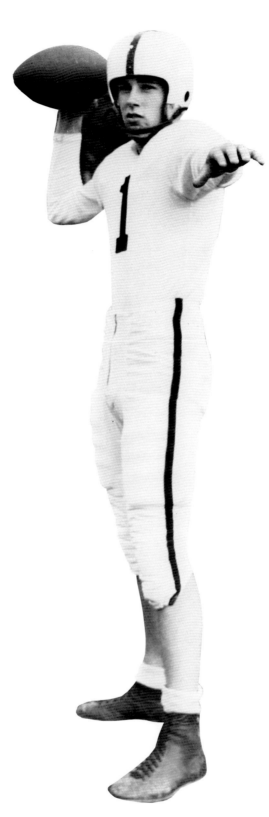

Left: *Charley Maloy
was a nifty
quarterback for
Anderson during the
early 1950s at Holy
Cross. In his first
game under
Anderson, he helped
the Crusaders to a
20-20 upset tie against
Dartmouth.*

Trophy when the season ended, while Anderson was named Coach of the Year.

Anderson had only so-so success thereafter at Iowa, still managing to spring an upset now and then, as when his team defeated second-ranked Wisconsin in 1942. When his request for tenure was rejected after the 1949 season, he returned to Holy Cross, where he always claimed to have the fondest memories. He also showed he had lost none of his magic, because he gave an untested sophomore quarterback, Charley Maloy, a tidy passing game and pulled off a 20-20 upset tie against favored Dartmouth in his first game. He upset powerful Syracuse 21-19 in 1957, and then spoiled their perfect season the following year with a 14-13 victory. In 1963, the Crusaders had won only one game as they prepared to meet heavily favored Boston College, their arch rival. But Anderson came up with special defenses to help contain the Eagles' mobile quarterback, Jack Con-

cannon, and his team came away with a stunning 9-0 upset.

Perhaps Holy Cross president Rev. John A. O'Brien, S. J., put it best when, in welcoming Anderson back for his second tour, he noted: "His personal character and integrity have added luster to the fine reputation of our team for good sportsmanship, fair play and gentlemanly conduct. He is the type of coach and man that we are proud to have for our boys."

DANA X. BIBLE

Record:

Miss. College (1913-15)	13-9-2
Louisiana State (1916)	3-0-2
Texas A&M (1917-27)	72-19-9
Nebraska (1928-36)	50-15-7
Texas-Austin (1937-46)	63-31-3

His middle name was Xenophon, and his mother's name was Cleopatra. The man himself, Dana X. Bible, was every bit as colorful as the monickers that were a part of his heritage.

Bible was forever linked by headline writers and pundits alike to The Good Book for most of the 34 seasons that he coached intercollegiate football at five schools. But that didn't bother him a whit, because when he wasn't spinning tales that appealed to all the good ol' boys from Nebraska to the Deep South, he was single-mindedly doing what he loved most of all – winning football games.

When he coached high school football at Brandon

Below: Dana Bible was an established winner when he went to Nebraska in 1928, having won 72 games at Texas A&M. He led the Cornhuskers to 50 victories and six conference titles in eight seasons.

Prep in Shelbyville, Tennessee, he dogged the heels of such great college coaches as Bob Zuppke, Pop Warner, Amos Alonzo Stagg, Fielding Yost (while he was trying to enrich himself by developing a Kentucky oil field); and Dr. Henry Williams, originator of the "Minnesota Shift," who showed him the very rocking chair he had sat in when he dreamed up his famed offense, and so impressed Bible that he adopted the offense for his own use.

When he applied for his first college coaching job at Mississippi College, the school's president led him to the chapel and told the students, "This is Mr. Bible, an applicant for our coaching position. Mr. Bible will now conduct chapel services." Caught unaware by the mandate, he read Scriptures, drew a homily from them and asked the president to give benediction. He also got the job.

He was just 21 years old, but looked twice that, with a smooth, bald head and a habit of smacking his lips as he discoursed on any serious matter in a voice that resembled a bullfrog. Nonetheless, he felt he could beat the world, and in his third season at Mississippi College, in 1915, he scheduled Tulane University, coached by another Williams disciple, Clark Shaughnessy. This was a classic overmatch, but Shaughnessy, always more caught up in theory than in the practical side, neglected to scout Bible's team, and got licked 20-8.

Meanwhile, Bible had agreed to coach the freshmen at Texas A&M, and before the 1916 season had expired, he had done such a good job that Louisiana State asked the Aggies to "borrow" him to replace their head coach, Irving Pray, who had left for military service in World War I. Bible won three and tied two of five games, and was asked to stay.

But Texas A&M knew a good coach when they saw him, and signed him to a three-year contract which eventually stretched from 1917 to 1927, during which he produced five of his 14 conference champions (eight would be in the unpredictable Southwest Conference.) Two championships came in his first three seasons, and those two teams didn't allow a point. His first three teams compiled a 26-1 record and scored 837 points to just seven by the opposition, one big reason why Bible never had a losing season with the Aggies.

Perhaps his most lasting contribution to Texas A&M came against Centre College in the Dixie Classic in Dallas on New Year's Day, 1922. Centre had gained national recognition that year by beating mighty Harvard 6-0, moving Bible to note, "Up to that time, Centre had done nothing more as a college than produce 26 college presidents, eight U.S. senators and 37 congressmen." Bible's Aggies were 20-point underdogs and he realized early in the game that he needed more running backs. Looking into the stands where the Cadet Corps was seated, Bible called for a trooper named King Gill. The Corps rose and cheered as Gill ran to don

his uniform, and though he never played that day as A&M upset Centre 22-14, the Corps was forever nicknamed "The Twelfth Man," and its members always stand up throughout every game.

By 1927, Bible had accomplished all he could at Texas A&M and he answered Nebraska's call for someone to resuscitate its program. Knute Rockne was offered the job first, but turned it down and recommended Bible, who then won six Big Six Conference titles in eight years. In a game against Indiana in 1936, the week after a heartbreaking loss to mighty Minnesota, the Huskers trailed 9-0 at the half, and Bible showed one of his finest attributes – his ability to get a team fired up. He challenged his team's manhood, and then offered the starting jobs to the first 11 men "who want to win badly enough" to be the first ones out of the locker room. There was a stampede to the door but Bible got there first, blocked the way and told his squad he didn't think it was "ready." In a flash, players began jos-

tling each other and soon there was a near-riot as players fought each other to get through the door. Nebraska then played the last half with 11 men and won 14-9.

In 1937, the University of Texas was at the bottom of the Southwest Conference and so desperate to revive its program that it agreed to give Bible a 10-year, $150,000 contract to be head coach and athletic director. This was an astounding amount in 1937, because most football coaches usually made far less than $10,000. Even Texas' president made just $10,000 a year, and its professors no more than $5,000. But the alumni forced the issue, and then agreed to double the president's salary, the first time that a football coach ever helped get his boss a raise.

Bible came to Austin with his now-famous "Bible Plan," which was nothing more than a program to mobilize alumni and high school coaches to funnel the state's best players to him so he could turn the

Above: *Bible (center) with two of his players at Texas A&M, where he coached from 1917 through 1927 after being "loaned" to LSU as a head coach in 1916.*

program around within five years. He guaranteed no immediate results, said he was no miracle worker and asked for time to do the job. He needed it because the banners of 1937 proclaiming "Bible-The Answer to Our Prayer," turned to "Ali Bible and His Forty Sieves" after his first two teams won just three games.

But the Bible Plan soon began reaping dividends and by 1941, the Longhorns had one of the most powerful teams in football history, led by Pete Layden and Jack Crain. It won eight of 10 games, scored 338 points but was tied by Baylor 7-7 and stunned the week after by TCU when Emory Nix's TD pass in the final minute gave TCU a 14-7 victory. In the next four seasons, Bible's teams won three conference titles, and won two and tied one in the Cotton Bowl. When he retired after the 1946 season to spend his final decade as the school's athletic director, he had won 63 games.

He also became a legend, and set a tone for football that, even a half century later, is the stuff for fiction writers. For example, Bible had asked Longhorns band director Colonel George Hurt to play "The Eyes of Texas," the anthem of the Lone Star State, whenever his team was struggling. When Arkansas led Texas 13-7 with 50 seconds to play in a 1939 game, Hurt's band played the song while the team took a time out. The team heard some 20,000 spectators singing and became so moved that on the first play, R. B. Patrick tossed a pass to Crain, who sidestepped his way through the entire Arkansas team for the winning touchdown.

After a scoreless tie against TCU while he coached at Texas A&M, his unhappy team was anxious to leave the stadium but the bus driver told an impatient player, "Take it easy bub. We got all night."

Bible jumped up and shouted, "Get this heap going or I'll jerk you out of that seat and take it myself."

Yet when his Aggies' team trailed SMU in 1925, he blasted them at halftime: "Listen, you farmers, if you don't go out there and beat those Methodists, don't come back in this doorway. Just climb the fence and go home." It didn't happen, and his team did just that – climbed the fence and walked back to their rooms.

When a Texas substitute left the game, every player on the bench stood. His captains always delivered the pep talks in their dorm and often before a game in the locker room while Bible stood by silently. His offenses never were spectacular, but there always was speed, one of the "Five S's" that keyed his teams' success – Spirit, Skill, Size and Savvy were the others.

All of this was good enough to make Dana Xenophon Bible one of the early inductees to the National Football Hall of Fame and a legend in a conference where football legends are truly beloved.

Below: *Dr. Henry Williams, inventor of the famed "Minnesota Shift," so impressed Bible that he adopted the offense.*

Below right: *Bible, seen here with son Bill, became Texas' athletic director after leading the team to 63 wins in 10 seasons.*

BERNIE BIERMAN

Record:

University of Montana (1919-21)	9-9-3
Mississippi State (1925-26)	8-8-1
Tulane (1927-31)	36-11-2
Minnesota (1932-41)	63-12-5
Minnesota (1945-49)	30-23-1

The Big Ten has often been portrayed as a group of teams more apt to steamroll opponents than dazzle them with speed and deception. More than any other Big Ten coach in history (Woody Hayes simply inherited the mantle), Bernie Bierman, the "Grey Fox" from Minnesota, was responsible for establishing this oft-imprecise picture, because his teams that won five national and six conference championships from 1932 to 1941 exuded an aura of tremendous strength and dominance. Think of the Big Ten in those days, and Minnesota's thumping, crunching style of football comes to mind.

It was often a dullish, straight-ahead approach to the game, even by standards back then (the Southwest Conference was famous at the time for its "aerial circus") but if ever a football philosophy fit the head coach's temperament, Bierman's beliefs were a mirror of the man. He was a stern taskmaster who became the nation's foremost proponent of single wing power, though he had once used the T-formation when he coached at Tulane University, and it was in his team's playbook at Minnesota, but rarely used.

Nor was it unusual for his teams to use only four or five plays for most of a game. This led friends and critics alike to often brand his football "dull," but his rejoinder always was that if something worked, why not continue to use it? "Besides," he once said, "we probably have more plays than any of our opponents. We just use the ones which work."

Bierman had learned the famed "Minnesota Shift" from his coach, Dr. Henry Williams, and later refined it with a buck-lateral system that complemented his basic single wing. Bierman's defenders often noted there was nothing dull about this offense, because the fullback headed into the line of scrimmage and then handed off the ball to the blocking back, whose options were to turn and run himself; hand it to a back going in another direction; or pitch it back to an end on a reverse. This first gained prominence when Minnesota defeated mighty Pitt 14-7 in 1934. Trailing 7-0 at the half, the Gophers tied the score early in the fourth quarter when Johnny Alphonse scored on a buck-lateral fake to Pug Lund, and then got the game-winner on

Left: *Bernie Bierman was the nation's foremost football coach during the 1930s, leading Minnesota to four national titles. The "Grey Fox" was as renowned for his lack of sentimentality as he was for his slug-it-out style of football.*

Lund's pass to Bob Tennor when Pitt's defense got mesmerized by the buck-lateral. That victory, above all others, finally focused national prominence on Bierman's team and led to the first of its

Above: *Bierman's 1934 national champions included future Hall of Fame coach Bud Wilkinson (third row, fourth from left), who was an offensive guard and blocking back. From 1934 through 1936, the Gophers lost just one game under Bierman.*

Right: *Bierman was captain of Minnesota's unbeaten 1915 team that won the Big Ten title. He adopted much of the style of football that he learned under his coach, Dr. Henry Williams.*

national championships.

Bierman never put much credence in variety offenses, just as he never made any secret about his sure-fire coaching methods. "There's nothing secret about the results to be obtained with blocking, tackling and hard charging. That's fundamental." That is why his teams nearly always controlled the second half of a game. During its undefeated championship 1941 season, Minnesota came from behind to win six times in nine games. One of them was the famous "talking play" against Northwestern. The Gophers trailed 7-2 in the second half when they sauntered to the line of scrimmage, and Bob Sweiger preoccupied the Wildcats by starting an argument. Suddenly, without a signal being called, the center simply flipped the ball to halfback Bud Higgins, and he ran 50 yards around his right end for the winning points while the "casual" Gophers blocked their men.

This all began on the practice field, where he was not always loved by his players. For example, the penalty for making a mistake was to jog once or twice around the field – not just the player who made the mistake, but the entire team. All of this was calculated to unify the players as a team,

another of Bierman's prized commandments. If they resented the discipline, they did so as a team and then often played their best games just to prove him wrong. "Better to have the boys hate me and win than like me and come home disappointed in themselves," he once said.

He proved that point before the last game of the 1941 season against Wisconsin, with an undefeated season and national championship on the line. First, a Bierman tongue-lashing didn't work on the cocky Gophers during the week's practice, so he made them run continuous 100-yard dashes for 45 minutes, and players dropped like flies. Then he capped the session with a 30-minute run around the field. "We were so mad at Bernie that we slaughtered Wisconsin, 41-6," one of his players later said.

While his players ran a gamut of emotions about their coach, Bierman was never flustered. It has been claimed with some truth that he never lost his temper, rarely raised his voice, never shed a tear, never appealed to sentiment and never used emotional gimmicks to fire up his teams. Just before a game against Vanderbilt, his team raced from the locker room. "Come back here," Bierman

Left: *Bierman was named to coach the 1936 College All-Stars in their annual game against the NFL champions. Seven of his 1935 national champions were named to the team that played a 7-7 tie against the Detroit Lions.*

Above: Ed Widseth was a Hall of Fame tackle on Bierman's national championship team during the mid-1930s. Other All-America players on those teams included backs Pug Lund and Andy Uram, end Frank Larson and guard Bill Bevan.

in three sports and was captain of the 1915 football team – the last to win a Big Ten title until his own 1934 team did it. In college Bierman also won the Western Conference Medal for excellence in scholarship and athletics.

His first head coaching job was at Montana, where his reputation for perfection probably began when he demanded that his players complete 50 passes in a row before practice could end – and he didn't even like the forward pass!

After a year off to work in business, Bierman joined his Minnesota teammate, Clark Shaughnessy, at Tulane before becoming head coach at Mississippi State in 1925, and two years later replaced Shaughnessy at Tulane. During his six seasons with the Green Wave, he won three straight Southern Conference titles, capped by his undefeated 1931 team meeting, and losing to, Southern California in the Rose Bowl.

Each year that he was at Tulane, Bierman brought his old coach, Doc Williams, to help in preseason coaching, and each year, Williams returned to Minnesota and urged the school to hire this talented alumnus as head coach. Bierman finally got the job in 1932, and in his second season, the Gophers, featuring future Hall of Famers Pug Lund, Ed Widseth and Bud Wilkinson, began a 28-game unbeaten streak, including 21 wins in a row, that covered three full seasons. It finally was broken midway through the 1936 season by Northwestern's 6-0 victory, the Gophers' only loss that season. But the Associated Press, in its first season of polling for a national champion, still named them Number 1.

Bierman always claimed that the 1934 team, his first to win all of its games and the Rockne Trophy as national champion, was the best, giving it a narrow edge over his undefeated national championship teams of 1940-41 that featured Heisman Trophy winner Bruce Smith, George Franck and Bill Daley. Those teams, plus the 1942 unit, won 17 games in a row, a streak that was finally ended by Iowa Pre-Flight – coached ironically by Marine Corps Maj. Bernie Bierman, who along with several other football coaches, had been called into the service to help the Navy conduct a college-level conditioning program for prospective pilots.

When Bierman returned in 1945, much had changed, including himself. His enthusiasm for coaching waned after seeing the horror of war. He had some great players like Clayton Tonnemaker and Leo Nomellini, but he stayed with the single wing in an era where everyone was shifting to the T-formation. Though he had four winning seasons during that post-war time, including a near-miss for a conference title in 1949, Bierman retired after the 1950 season. Several years later, the "Silver Fox" was elected to the Hall of Fame, and Minnesota football still celebrates his success.

ordered, and they did. "Now walk – don't run – onto that field," he told them. "Do your warming up out there, not on the way. Keep your brains quiet. Your legs will take care of themselves."

But he wasn't exactly an iceberg, either. Before a game against Georgia, when he was coaching at Tulane, one of his assistant coaches finished a fiery appeal to the players by flinging his hat to the floor and screaming, "I can lick the whole state of Georgia myself!" Bierman shoved forward, smashed his own heel into that hat and said, almost in a whisper, "So can I."

Bierman really never asked his players to endure anything he hadn't also endured. He had three operations as a child to cure osteomyelitis, then starred in three sports at Litchfield (Minnesota) High School. At Minnesota, he won seven letters

EARL (RED) BLAIK

Record:

Dartmouth (1934-40) 45-15-4
Army (1941-58)   121-33-10

The letter was addressed to Lt. Earl H. Blaik, and delivered to the Army post at Fort Bliss, Texas. It was from Maj. Gen. Douglas MacArthur, and it invited Lt. Blaik, who MacArthur had known when he was superintendent at West Point a few years earlier and Blaik was a star athlete, to become his personal aide.

In one of those mind-boggling quirks of fate, Lt. Blaik had departed the post – and the Army – the day before and was en route home to Dayton, Ohio, to help run his family's construction business. Thus by the slim margin of 24 hours did college football gain the lifetime services of one of its

greatest coaches. And in ironic compensation, the Army became the ultimate beneficiary, as Blaik became the greatest coach in West Point history.

While West Point and Dartmouth both claim him for their own, Blaik really was a product of the "Cradle of Coaches," Miami University in Oxford, Ohio where he played football for coach George Little, was captain of the baseball team, president of the student body and anchor man on the debating team. With World War I underway when he graduated in 1918, Blaik entered West Point, allowed under rules of that time, and graduated two years later under an accelerated wartime program. He competed in four sports, and besides being selected as the best athlete in his class, he was listed among the ends on Walter Camp's prestigious All-America team.

Football had no place in his life for a couple of years after his Army career until Little, then head coach at Wisconsin, invited him in 1924 to help with pre-season training. Three years later, he returned to West Point as an assistant coach, and

Above: *Red Blaik was an assistant coach at West Point before becoming head coach at Dartmouth in 1934. He returned to Army in 1941.*

Right: *One of Blaik's most famous pupils at West Point was running back Red Cagle, who Blaik ranked as one of the best he ever coached.*

Right: *Red Friesell was the referee in the famed "fifth down" game between Blaik's Dartmouth team and unbeaten Cornell in 1940. The Big Red scored an apparent winning TD on an extra play, but when the error was discovered after the game, they renounced the TD and the win.*

during eight seasons, among other achievements, tutored the second-best backfield duo in Army history, Red Cagle and Harry Wilson. Twenty years later he had the best – Doc Blanchard and Glenn Davis.

Though he did not even seek the job, Dartmouth named Blaik as its first non-graduate head coach in 1934 (he later became the first non-active-duty coach at West Point) and he brought the program from the depths of oblivion to a pair of outright Ivy League titles in 1936 and 1937, and a shared title with Cornell in 1938, once compiling an unbeaten string of 22 games. He is probably best remembered at Dartmouth for the famous "fifth down" game against top-ranked Cornell in 1940 when referee Red Friesell mistakenly awarded the Big Red an extra down that became a winning touchdown pass in the final six seconds of an apparent 7-3 victory. But when game films revealed the discrepancy, Cornell offered to nullify the score, and the victory that cost them the national title.

In 1940, Army football, which had traditionally been handled by active duty officers, had produced just four victories in two seasons. Superintendent

Right: *Blaik was renowned for turning out future head coaches from his Army staff. Vince Lombardi (fourth from left) coached for him for five seasons before joining the NFL. Other future head coaches from that staff included Murray Warmuth and Paul Amen (sixth and seventh from left) who later coached at Minnesota and Wake Forest, respectively.*

Left: *Blaik was the first non-graduate ever hired as head football coach at Darmouth, and brought the Big Green its first-ever Ivy League titles in 1936 and 1937, and a shared title in 1938. Those three teams won 21 and lost just three games.*

Above: *Many believe
Blaik's 1944 team was
the greatest in college
football history. He
had two complete
backfields, including
one that included (left
to right) Tom
Lombardo, Dean
Sensanbaugher, Doc
Blanchard and Glenn
Davis. Blanchard and
Davis became the most
famous backfield duo
in the game's history.*

Maj. Gen. Robert Eichelberger, during a previous tour at West Point in the 1930s, had tried unsuccessfully to change the system so Blaik could get the job. Now that he was boss, he hired Blaik, breaking for all time the officer-coach tradition. Breaking any tradition in the Army is risky business, but there never were any regrets, because West Point enjoyed unparalleled success during Blaik's 19-year tenure.

He is probably best remembered as the leader of Army's marvelous teams that, from 1944-46, featured Doc Blanchard and Glenn Davis, "Mr. Outside" and "Mr Inside," the most powerful offensive pairing in college football history. Those teams never lost a game, won two national championships, three of his seven Eastern titles and produced 10 of his 33 first-team All-America players, including a pair of Heisman Trophy winners in Blanchard and Davis. Their victims included fine Notre Dame teams by scores of 59-0 and 48-0, and three victories over Navy, which for two years was as powerful as Army and previously had beaten West Point for five straight years – a grim situation for any Army football coach.

Less than a decade later, after Blaik's teams had

enjoyed two more unbeaten seasons and a 28-game unbeaten string, he saw his great program decimated by a suspected "cribbing scandal" that had its roots among some top brass who had become "embarrassed" by Army's football success. It wiped out nearly every football letterman, including his own son, Bob, and Blaik would have left West Point had not MacArthur, his dearest friend, urged him "not to quit under fire, to fight them until you bring them to their knees."

Three years later, Blaik rebuilt Army football to championship status and capped his career in 1958 with his sixth unbeaten Army season that also produced an Eastern title and a third Heisman winner, Pete Dawkins.

During World War II, Blaik was fortunate to have some great talent on his teams. Wartime rules allowed many of the nation's best players to enroll at the two major service academies. His 1944 team had two separate units – "alternate teams," Blaik called them – and Blanchard and Davis were on the second unit. Blaik said that the best game he ever saw occurred one Wednesday afternoon on The Plain when those units scrimmaged each other, and each of them scored two touchdowns.

"It was one of the most vicious as well as beautifully coordinated exhibitions of team football that I ever saw," he later said. The 1944 Army team was the first to win all its games since 1916, and averaged 56 points a game. After Army defeated Navy, the nation's Number 2 team, 23-7, among the messages Blaik received was one that read: "We have stopped the war to celebrate your magnificent success. MacArthur."

Even with the awesome depth and power of the 1944 team, Blaik called his 1945 team the best he ever saw at West Point – "a dream team" – with quarterback Arnold Tucker directing the Blanchard-Davis backfield. But those teams were exceptions because young men don't go to West Point for athletics, and in subsequent years, Blaik was a master of extracting the very best from available talent. When Army was en route home by train after being walloped by Notre Dame 27-7 in 1947 at South Bend, Blaik told his players, "Get this game out of your minds before you get off this train. We were defeated by a better team and the question

now is one of resolve for the future. We'll face two sure defeats from Pennsylvania and Navy unless we rise to our best effort, and you alone can turn a bleak future into a great season."

The next week, Army tied favored Penn and then rolled over Navy 21-0. For years Blaik showed the film of that game as the perfect example of how an Army team should prepare itself for Navy.

In 1955, he had no experienced quarterbacks, so he switched an All-America end, Don Holleder, to the position, and both endured almost constant criticism. But Blaik supplied him with a crunching running game, and allowed Holleder's great athletic and competitive instincts to do the rest, helping the Cadets to a 7-1-1 record, including a 20-7 upset victory over Navy – and beating Navy was the ultimate goal of that risky venture.

He also showed his great ability as an innovator by developing the "lonely end" offense for his unbeaten team in 1958, always keeping an end, usually Bill Carpenter, flanked to the outside. He

Below: The "game of the 1940s" matched Blaik's great Blanchard and Davis team against unbeaten Notre Dame. The 1946 game ended in a scoreless tie. Here, Davis carries for a seven-yard gain.

Above: *Blaik's Army teams were among the best nationally during the 1940s. His 1950 team extended an unbeaten string to 28 games from 1947 while his 1944-46 teams, featuring Blanchard and Davis, did not lose a game in their three seasons.*

didn't even come into the huddle, but got his plays from a series of foot and hand signals when quarterback Joe Caldwell stood in the huddle.

Formations and great players notwithstanding, Blaik's prime commandment for success was total preparation. "I never believed that the bounce of the ball determined a game's outcome," he said. "It's what is done in preparation. These things are the essence of success."

This philosophy was one great reason why Blaik's teams came up with upset after upset. Even in his first season, 1941, when he was just beginning to reorganize the football program, he achieved a scoreless tie against a superior Notre Dame team. He shocked a favored Michigan team in 1946 when quarterback Arnold Tucker could not even lift his arm to pass, and had to toss the ball back to Davis any time Army wished to throw the ball; and then twice more upset Wolverine Rose Bowl champions in the next four years. Dozens of his former players became general officers, some attaining the Army's highest command positions. Nineteen of his coaches, including Vince Lombardi, distinguished themselves as pro or college head coaches. Blaik was elected to the Hall of Fame, and later received the National Football Foundation's Gold Medal for his contributions to the sport. He died in 1989 at age 92.

BOBBY BOWDEN

Record:

Samford (1959-62)	31-6-0
West Virginia (1970-75)	42-26-0
Florida State (1976-89)	122-40-3*
*Still active	

Forty-two seconds were left on the clock at Florida State's Campbell Stadium on the second Saturday of 1987, and a jammed house of more than 60,000 fans were on their feet, screaming, yelling – and probably praying.

Florida State, unbeaten in four games, had just scored a touchdown to draw within a point of the University of Miami, unbeaten in two games, 26-25. The game's winner could have a shot at Number 1 in the polls and a leg up in the race to the national championship. On the sidelines, Florida State coach Bobby Bowden had to make a decision. Should he kick the extra point and settle for a hard-fought tie? After all, his team had trailed 26-19 with 2:22 to play, and had played a heroic game against the Hurricanes. A tie would not be a disgrace, and both teams could then fight it out for a top spot for the remainder of the season.

On the other hand, kicker Derek Schmidt had already missed an extra point – the difference in the game – and a pair of relatively easy field goals; and another field goal try had been botched without the kick even being attempted. Bowden decided to go for the victory, and called for a pass from quarterback Danny McManus to end Pat Carter.

However, Bowden's grand plan was spoiled when Miami defensive back Bubba McDowell knocked down the pass, and the Hurricanes came away with a win and eventually won the national championship with a perfect record while the Seminoles finished second with their 11-1 mark after beating Nebraska in the Fiesta Bowl.

Bowden has endured such close shaves – he's won a few, too – for all of his life because that is how his team plays its game. He may be a quiet, composed and very reachable person away from the game, but when his team plays, he has it attacking and often doing outlandish things. The Seminoles rarely play a dull game.

Often, the feelings are contagious. In 1988, Florida State was ranked Number 1 in several pre-season polls, the first time in the school's relatively short gridiron history that it had ever been top-ranked in anything. They were scheduled to play Miami in the first game of the season, and many believed a national champion could emerge from this game. But so disdainful were the Seminoles of the defending national champions that they recorded a rap video the week before the game, boasting that Miami could not defeat them this time. Final score: Miami 31, Florida State 0.

"We thought we could just walk out and win," Bowden said later. "It doesn't work that way."

What has always "worked" for Bowden, though, is a wide-open style of offense that is just as effective home or away. In fact, Bowden has gained a reputation for being a fine "road coach" because he won more than two-thirds of his away games, as well as some 82 per cent of the home games. Where he plays doesn't seem to matter. He's gone into the noisy pit of Bayou Bengal country at LSU and won four of five games; he is 3-1 at South Carolina, and unbeaten at such partisan locales as Notre Dame and Ohio State.

What makes his football so interesting is his penchant for always making a gadget play or two available in every game. In 1988, for example, his team was tied with Clemson in the Tigers' famed "Death Valley" stadium, and faced a 4th-and-21 situation with 79 seconds to play. With all 84,000 fans in the stadium and a national television audience expecting a punt, Bowden had another idea, one he had carefully choreographed with his center, punter and punt blockers. Punter Tim Corlew faked get-

Below: *Bobby Bowden is the second winningest active Division 1-A coach, with 195 victories through the 1989 season, including 122 during his 14 seasons at Florida State.*

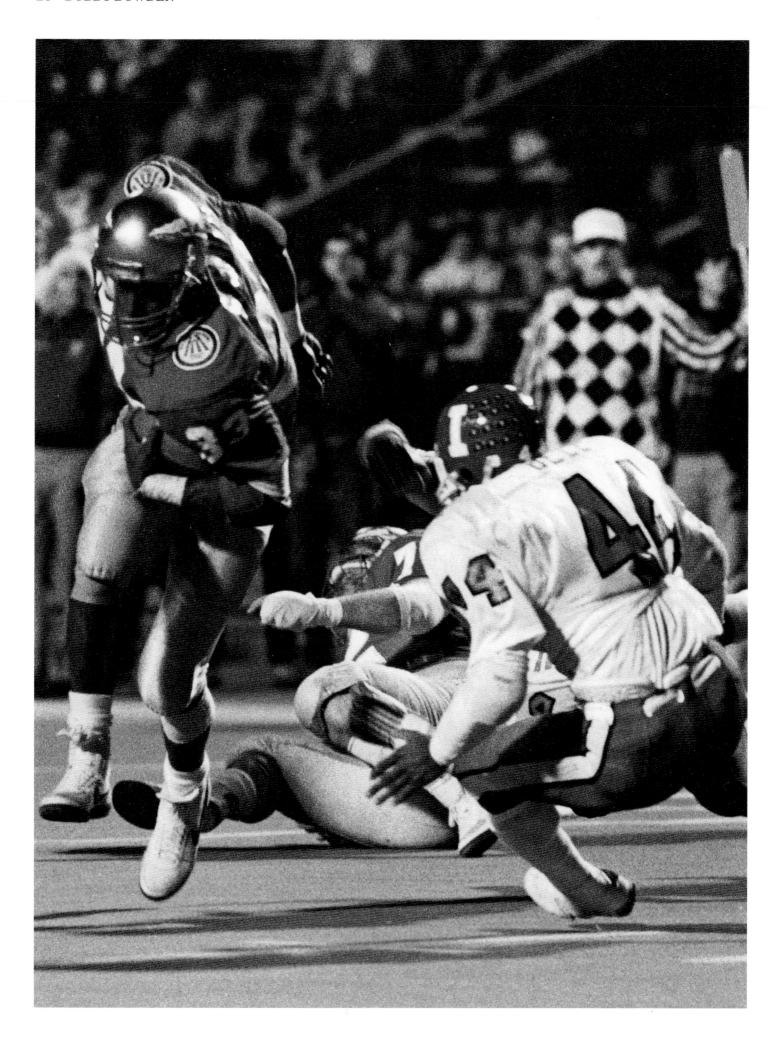

Above: *Bowden's teams have been great "finishers," and during the 1980s his teams won six bowl games, including a thrilling 31-28 victory over Nebraska in the 1988 Fiesta Bowl. Here, Florida State's Edgar Bennett rolls for a big gain.*

Opposite: *Bowden has had great running backs at Florida State but none better than Sammie Smith, who became the school's all-time rusher. Here, he moves for a big gain in a 1986 game against Indiana as the Hoosiers' Leonard Bell comes in for the tackle.*

ting a high snap, drawing the eager Clemson punt rusher past blocker LeRoy Butler. But the ball went to another blocker, Dwayne Williams, who then handed it to Butler, who raced 78 yards down the left sideline to Clemson's 1-yard line. A short time later, Florida State kicked the game-winning field goal.

"It was the old 'Puntrooskie'," a delighted Bowden said afterward, adding: "It was the dumbest thing I ever did."

On November 1, 1986 at the Orange Bowl, Miami had just scored to take a 14-7 lead late in the opening quarter, but Bowden decided not to wait for any gamble. He wanted to try to even the score right away. On the ensuing kickoff, Keith Ross took the ball in the end zone before running right to the 15-yard line. He was surrounded by Miami tacklers and threw a lateral across the field to speedy Dexter Carter, who ran untouched for the tie-making score. In the end the fancy play didn't help, because Miami crushed the Seminoles 41-23, but the Hurricanes certainly hadn't won in a relaxed manner.

Bowden has proven since he arrived at Florida State from West Virginia in 1976 that he is at his best when his back is to the wall. Six times in 14

years his team won 10 or more games, and he has taken his teams to 11 post-season games.

He admits to being a "speed freak" with his teams, which helps him achieve his goal of wide-open football. He gained his edge in offensive football during his three seasons as a quarterback at Howard College (now Samford University) in Birmingham, Alabama, after one year at the University of Alabama. He earned Little All-America honors and six years after graduating, he returned as head coach for a four-year tour. Coincidentally, his son Terry also became head coach at Samford, and was joined by another son and son-in-law.

Bowden was head coach at West Virginia for five years, during which his teams averaged almost 30 points a game, and he went to Florida State in 1976 to inherit a team that had been 4-29 over the three previous seasons. He had a 5-6 record in his first season, but won his last three games when plays of 80 or more yards in each game decided matters. His teams appeared in eight straight bowl games from 1982 to 1988, two after 11-1 seasons.

"There are no secrets," he said of his success. "We keep our mouths shut and go about our business because our backs are to the wall in every game."

PAUL (BEAR) BRYANT

Record:

Maryland (1945)	6-2-1
Kentucky (1946-53)	60-23-5
Texas A&M (1954-57)	25-14-2
Alabama (1958-82)	232-46-9

His reign of power
From his tower,
Bear Bryant,
The Gridiron King.

So went a popular folk ballad in Alabama about the coach who won more major college games than anyone in intercollegiate history, and whose career was worthy of folk ballads which celebrate legends, real or imagined.

Everything about Bryant was legendary, beginning with his nickname, forged when he was just 17 years old in Fordyce, Arkansas and was pushed into a ring to wrestle a live bear for a dollar a minute as part of a sideshow stunt in a travelling carnival. The legend grew to Bunyonesque proportions, but Bryant admitted, "He looked mighty big to me, but he was probably a scrawny thing. His muzzle came off right away, and I got out of the ring."

That might have been the only time in his life that Bryant backed down. His legend was built around such heroics as once completing a game for Alabama against Mississippi State with a broken leg, and then throwing away his crutches to play an entire game the following week. Bryant was a member of the Tide's 1934 unbeaten team that defeated Stanford in the Rose Bowl – the "other end," opposite the great pass catcher, Don Hutson.

While Hutson went on to greater glory in the pros, Bryant became an assistant to Alabama coach Frank Thomas, and then worked at Vanderbilt before entering the Navy to coach football at North

Right: *Bear Bryant is the winningest coach in Division 1-A football, with 323 victories at four schools. His Alabama teams won 232 games, and added six national titles and 13 SEC crowns. When he finished coaching in 1982, he was to Alabama football what Knute Rockne was to Notre Dame.*

Carolina Pre-Flight in the V-project that conditioned future Navy pilots. After the war, he resisted George Preston Marshall's offer to coach his Washington Redskins, so Marshall got him the head coaching job at the University of Maryland, just five days before the 1945 season began. He took 17 players from his Pre-Flight team with him and won six of nine games, but left after one season because he and Maryland's president, Curly Byrd, disagreed on the school's firing of an assistant coach.

Kentucky had won just two games in 1945, and it answered Bryant's desire to return to the Southeastern Conference. He produced some of Kentucky's greatest teams – and nearly a half-century later still was their winningest coach – as the Wildcats won three of four bowl games, including a stunning upset over top-ranked Oklahoma in the 1950 Sugar Bowl when Bryant devised a 3-4 defense that cut down the Sooners' famed split-T attack. Coach Bud Wilkinson was so impressed that he swapped some of his split-T secrets for the intricacies of that defense, then used it so successfully that it became known as the "Oklahoma defense."

It is hard to imagine Bryant finishing second to

Above: *Bryant (seated, center) had revitalized football at Texas A&M during the mid-1950s when he decided to return to his alma mater, and signed a 10-year contract in 1958. He is seen here with his wife Mary (right), trustee Ernest Williams (seated, left) and ex-Alabama star Fred Sington.*

Left: *Bryant had great teams at the University of Kentucky that featured a passing attack of Babe Parilli to end Steve Meilinger (right), as well as a defense that shut down Oklahoma's Wing-T in the 1950 Sugar Bowl.*

Above: *Bryant's Alabama teams were hot draws in post-season games, and appeared in 23 consecutive bowls during 24 straight winning seasons. His 1963 team defeated Mississippi 12-7 in the Sugar Bowl and carried Bryant off the field.*

anyone, but he couldn't overcome the power of Adolph Rupp, Kentucky's legendary basketball coach, and despite having signed a 12-year contract, he left the school in 1954 to resuscitate Texas A&M's program. He did this the hard way – at least as far as the Aggies' players were concerned – because he took two busloads of them to a God-forsaken barrenness named Junction, Texas. Only one busload returned, with 27 players who had endured weeks of twice-daily practices during one of the hottest, driest periods in the state's history. All seemed for naught when his first team won just one of ten games – the only losing season

he ever had – but the Aggies lost only four games in the next three seasons, with an undefeated season and Southwest Conference title in 1956 and a Gator Bowl appearance (3-0 loss to Tennessee) in 1957.

His Aggie team had been placed on a two-year probation by the Southwest Conference for recruiting violations – the last time Bryant ever incurred such a penalty – and the alumni were unhappy about having been cut out of the decision-making. Alabama, meanwhile, had sunk to the depths of the SEC, so with the immortal words, "I heard mama calling me home," Bryant returned to his alma mater in 1958. There he became an

he always let it be known that "I still know a whole lot about coaching people." His mere presence was as important as any play he ever sent in, and there never was a murmur of discontent as Bryant spent more and more energy fighting his own private war against Stagg's image. "I thought I was strong enough to handle it," he said. "But I was wrong." He refused to discuss it publicly until he tied Stagg's mark by beating Penn State, the week before the final game of the 1981 season against Auburn. Then he said he wanted to get it for his players – and they, of couse, wanted it for him. Both got what they wanted. He coached one more year before admitting that the job had grown too heavy, winning his last game against Illinois in the Liberty Bowl.

What was football to Bear Bryant?

"It's not a game, it's life," he said. "It teaches discipline, sacrifice and hard work. The true star is the man who works for the team."

He developed team spirit with his insistence that players should "hit, and hit hard," constantly urging them to "suck up your guts and knock 'em out of there." But he never tolerated dirty football, and players who couldn't distinguish between hard and dirty play simply did not play.

Bryant knew how to inspire a team with just a few words – and his physical presence. He was a

Above: Quarterback Joe Namath was the star of Bryant's 1964 national championship team at Alabama, but even Namath felt the sting of Bear's wrath when he was suspended during his junior year for rules infractions. Namath later said that Bryant was like a father to him.

Overleaf: Bryant's Alabama teams were always totally prepared, and they were equally talented on defense as on offense. In this 1967 action, the Tide causes Ole Miss to fumble.

almighty ruler who brought the school to never-imagined heights in the sport, and Bryant to the pinnacle of his profession. When he retired at age 69 after the 1982 season, he surpassed the immortal Amos Alonzo Stagg's lifetime record of 314 victories with his own 323 career wins, 232 of them at Tuscaloosa, and a litany of achievements that included six national championships, 13 SEC titles, 23 consecutive bowl appearances and 24 straight winning seasons.

Bryant pursued Stagg's record ardently, and he admitted that his assistants carried most of the coaching load during the last few seasons, though

Above: *Bryant was renowned for developing fine quarterbacks. Ken Stabler (12) followed Joe Namath at Alabama and joined other fine QBs as Steve Sloan, Scott Hunter and Jeff Rutledge.*

Above right: *Another Alabama victory, and a jubilant Crimson Tide team carries the Bear off the field once more.*

great organizer, but for years he had a dozen assistants to help him, though he always gave them credit for winning, and took the blame for a loss; and he was a perfectionist in his insistence on error-free play.

Bryant was definitely the boss. He was an imposing physical specimen at six feet, four inches, with a craggy face and a low, deep voice that was half growl, half speech that often was unfathomable to listeners, but which still elicited instant attention. When he came down from his famous coaching tower that overlooked the Tide's practice field, coaches coached harder, players played harder, and managers even managed harder. He once suspended All-America quarterback Joe Namath for a couple of games because he broke training rules; and when another star was "dogging it" in practice, he ordered the team's managers to find "the dirtiest, filthiest, grimiest uniform, put it on him and make him earn a better one." When the player sassed him, Bryant literally threw him off the field and wouldn't reinstate him until the boy's father brought his son in for a meeting. The player later became All-America, and Bryant knew the potential was there. But he wouldn't allow anyone to give

less than a full effort, and this was a season (1966) when his unbeaten team won a national title.

Bryant always prided himself on keeping an "open door" to all of his players, regardless of a player's status on the team, and some of them said "he was like a father to us." Yet, not until his 1970 team got hammered badly by Southern Cal and its black fullback, Sam Cunningham, and other southern schools had begun to recruit black players, did he follow suit. His defenders claim with some merit that for most of the 1960s, state policies forbade Bryant from scheduling teams using black players or recruiting them for his team. Once he changed his policies, he won three more national titles and another 130 games, and his teams were models of racial harmony because Bryant never relented on one of his basic principles: "I told all kids that if they weren't a special kind of person, I didn't want them at Alabama."

Bryant always had said that when he stopped coaching football, he would probably die. This was sadly prophetic, because a month after coaching his final game, he passed away. Soon thereafter, he was elected to the Hall of Fame, which long before had reserved a spot for him.

JERRY CLAIBORNE

Record:

Virginia Tech (1961-70) 61-32-9
Maryland (1972-81)   77-37-3
Kentucky (1982-89)   41-46-3

Jerry Claiborne has proven that student-athletes can indeed be as successful in the classroom as they can be on the gridiron – in fact, he seems to have insisted upon it in the course of ranking fourth in victories among active Division 1-A coaches until his retirement in 1989. For that reason, he deserves to be enshrined among the best who have ever coached in college football.

Claiborne may never be recognized as a great creator of magic when he put X's and O's on the blackboard, though for most of his career he was among the best defensive practitioners in the game. But the way he melded the student-athlete with the athlete-student could be a model for others in the profession for years to come. He believed that to be successful on the field, players must have the brainpower to master the mental aspects of the game, which are at least as important as the physical aspects. He then encouraged

Below: *In Jerry Claiborne's second and third seasons at Kentucky, he brought his teams to the Hall of Fame Bowl, and got a free ride on his players' shoulder after beating Wisconsin in the second trip.*

Above: *One of the best players ever developed by Claiborne was Randy White, who played defensive line at Maryland and won the Outland Award in 1974, given to the nation's best collegiate lineman. White later became one of the greatest defensive linemen in NFL history while playing for the Dallas Cowboys.*

them to apply that same mental power when they stepped into the classroom.

In 1982, Claiborne inherited a University of Kentucky football program that was under fire regarding its lack of devotion to academics, and he pushed 90 percent of the incoming freshmen in his first and second seasons to get their degrees. No other major football program in the nation matched that figure. He was not concerned that his team didn't win a game in his first season, because for the next several seasons he had everything on the right track, and even had a pair of Hall of Fame Bowl appearances. The same thing had happened in his first head coaching job at Virginia Tech, and he took that school to its only Southern Conference championship two years later as well as to a pair of appearances in the Liberty Bowl; and again in his second job, at the University of Maryland, which had suffered through five head coaches, a 60-100-1 record in the previous 16 years, and hadn't been to a post-season game since Jim Tatum's great 1955 team visited the Orange Bowl. When Claiborne departed College Park in 1981 afer 10 years as head coach, his teams had won 77 games and had played

in seven post-season games.

Yet, Claiborne was more proud of the fact that he developed three Academic All-America players during that time, including his own son Jonathan, who was a walk-on candidate and wound up as a starting safety on Maryland's 11-0 regular season team in 1976 that went to the Cotton Bowl, and on the 1977 team that was 8-4 with an appearance in the Hall of Fame Bowl. He also had 34 players who were on the All-Atlantic Coast Conference Academic Football Team during that time. After becoming head coach at Kentucky in 1982, the Wildcats were atop the Southeastern Conference Academic Honor Roll with 51 selections. To prove that not by books alone do college football players survive, all of the academic stars he helped turn out at his three coaching stops also contributed to 11 of his teams which appeared in bowl games.

Claiborne had the unique ability to undertake a football and coaching education under Bear Bryant while maintaining a strong focus on academics. He played for Bryant's Kentucky teams of the late 1940s, ending his college career as a starting safety on the Wildcats' Orange Bowl team in 1949 and being named the team's Outstanding Senior. He established his own personal academic leanings in those years, too, because he was selected as Outstanding Senior in the College of Education and graduated from Kentucky with high distinction, accumulating a 2.7 grade point average out of a possible 3.0. Two decades later, he was elected to the University of Kentucky Hall of Fame.

Bryant's teams at that time had great firepower from quarterback Vito (Babe) Parilli, but were even stronger defensively, and Claiborne learned those lessons well because, after two years as a successful high school coach in Virginia, Bryant hired him as a defensive assistant. He worked for him during the rest of his tenure at Kentucky, and for three seasons was The Bear's defensive coordinator at Texas A&M, helping the Aggies to win the Southwest Conference title in just the second year of Bryant's regime. He joined Bryant again at Alabama as defensive coordinator after a year on Frank Broyles' staff at Missouri, and the Crimson Tide posted a three-year mark of 20-7-5, with a pair of bowl appearances, when Virginia Tech hired him as head coach.

After his success at Virginia Tech, Maryland was waiting with open arms for someone who could bring consistent success to its football program, which had known little since Tatum departed after 1955. By the time Claiborne had finished, the Terps had won three conference championships, their first since 1955, and enjoyed their first unbeaten season since that year as well. Maryland lost to Houston in the Cotton Bowl following the 1976 season, just as Tatum's unbeaten team had lost to Oklahoma in the Orange Bowl after its perfect 1955 regular season. While the 1976 team's performance was unique, Claiborne was more widely recognized for the job he did in his third season, 1974, when the Terps were 8-4 and shut out five opponents.

Claiborne also developed Outland Award and Lombardi Trophy winner Randy White, later a great NFL defensive lineman with the Dallas Cowboys, as well as All-Americans Joe Campbell, another defensive player, and kickers Nick Mick-Mayer and Dale Castro. Prior to Claiborne's arrival, the Terps had five All-ACC players in the previous seven seasons; when he left, nearly 40 had been accorded such honors.

When he moved to Kentucky in 1982, optimism was high at the prospect of an old grad coming home, but he ran into a schedule ranked Number 2 in the nation in degree of difficulty and tied only one of 11 games. However, Claiborne worked his magic the next season and the Wildcats roared to a 5-1 start and, for the first time since 1976, finished with an invitation to the Hall of Fame Bowl. His team tied Memphis State for honors as the nation's Most Improved Team.

Only two Kentucky coaches ever had teams that had six consecutive seasons with at least five victories in each season – Claiborne and his mentor, Bear Bryant. That's not bad company, but Claiborne goes the immortal Bear one better. His teams were also honored for their winning ways in the classroom.

Below: *Claiborne emphasized education with football, and saw 90 percent of his two frosh teams at Kentucky get their degrees. His 1989 team, shown here, was his last.*

DAN DEVINE

Record:

Arizona State (1955-57)   27-3-1
Missouri (1958-70)   93-37-7
Notre Dame (1975-80)   53-16-1

Below: Dan Devine replaced Ara Parseghian as head coach at Notre Dame in 1975, and two years later led the Irish to a national championship.

Dan Devine was a self-admitted "fuss-budget" when he coached at Arizona State, Missouri and Notre Dame. He also won 173 games in 21 seasons at those schools, so it is reasonable to assume that one man's "fuss-budget" becomes another man's winner.

A coach's teams are a reflection of his own personality, and while Devine turned out winning teams in 21 of his 22 college seasons, those 173 victories didn't seem to have the same lasting ring as those of Knute Rockne, Woody Hayes and Bear Bryant. Devine won some very big and very thrilling games under the glare of a national spotlight,

yet his victories can best be described as "quiet successes," because he was a quiet, almost bland person, who on first meeting seemed to lack any outward fire. His soft-spoken, sometimes apologetic and monotonous style accentuated his perceived standoffishness. He was best described by a close friend as "what he is not – he is not a fiery type, but he is nobody's patsy; he is not a high-pressure recruiter, yet is an effective one; he is not an original football thinker, but nevertheless is a coach whose diversified tactics keep opponents guessing."

Ironically, Devine's football education was wrapped around the colorful multiple-offense theories of Biggie Munn and Duffy Daugherty at Michigan State, where he served as an assistant coach for five years. Devine embraced a system that included the best parts of the single wing, wing-T, double wing, and flanker formations, and used them so successfully in his first head coaching job at Arizona State that in his third and final season in the job, his team was unbeaten for the first time in the school's history and led the NCAA with 297 points in 10 games.

Before Devine came to the school, which had won only nine games in the previous two seasons, it was a poor second cousin to the University of Arizona in Tucson. It couldn't even recruit any of the top 11 high school seniors in the state. In Devine's first year, he got 10 of the best 11; the year after, he won nine of 10 games; and in his final season, he won all 10.

Devine was welcomed at Missouri – he was the only candidate interviewed for the job – where he replaced Frank Broyles, who had moved on to begin a very successful career at Arkansas. Broyles had built his teams on an iron-clad defense and a good punting game that included more quick-kicks than Tigers fans liked to watch. Broyles contended that lack of talent forced that style – and his departure – but three seasons later, the nucleus of Missouri's 1960 Big Eight champions were 13 players who Devine inherited when he took the job in 1958.

In his second season, the Tigers had a 6-4 record, then lost to Georgia, 14-0, in the Orange Bowl. That, Devine maintained, set the stage for his championship season "because our kids outplayed Georgia's big, rough Southeastern Conference champions and convinced themselves they belonged on the field with any team."

The way Devine coached his team and interacted with his players, whatever his personality, also had much to do with this success, and with subsequent successes at both Missouri and Notre Dame. He took the drudgery out of practice with relatively short workouts in which he ran his players hard but did away with the dull wind sprints afterwards because he preferred to take a chance

UNIVERSITY OF MISSOURI 1960

Above: *Devine led Missouri to its first bowl victory in the 1960 Orange Bowl over Navy. His Missouri teams won three bowl games in four tries.*

Right: *Devine's offense did a bit of everything, and at Missouri his best running back was Johnny Roland (left), an All-America selection.*

on not being fully prepared and have his players fresh rather than have them fully prepared and tired. He spent time with them, often at the training table, letting all know that he was approachable, and causing former Missouri coach Don Farout to note: "As good as he is at handling a team on the field, he's even better handling it off the field. Morale and conduct are never a problem."

Devine also let his players know that while he might forgive a fumble during a game because it was a physical mistake, he could never tolerate carelessness, failure to pursue on defense, to block downfield, or "to behave at all times like a football team." He also adapted his tactics to his material, once utilizing stocky little quarterback Ron Taylor at Missouri as a blocker every time he pitched the ball back to a halfback on a sweep. Taylor simply joined with two guards and the other two backs as blockers. Watching those tactics crush his Air Force team, Ben Martin coined the phrase long attributed to Southern California football when he said, "Devine gets so many blockers in front of the ball carrier, that he ought to call the play 'Student Body Left' or 'Student Body Right.'"

Devine's 1960 Missouri team had a perfect season spoiled by a clean-cut 23-7 loss to Kansas, but

recruiting violations later changed the loss to a forfeit victory. Still, Devine came away with a 21-14 victory in the Orange Bowl over a favored Navy team that had Heisman Trophy winner Joe Bellino. It was the school's first bowl win in seven tries, and Devine won three of four more appearances.

Devine left Missouri to become head coach and general manager of the Green Bay Packers from 1971 to 1974, but an NFL player's strike in 1974 soured him on pro football, and his inability to reincarnate Vince Lombardi's success soured Green Bay fans on him. Notre Dame offered him the head coaching job for the third time in his life in 1975, when Ara Parseghian was forced to retire for health reasons, and he took it. Though he won 53 games in six seasons, three of four post-season games, and the 1977 national championship when his team upset top-ranked Texas 38-10 in the Cotton Bowl, he was never embraced in the same manner at Notre Dame as were Rockne, Leahy and Parseghian.

His crowning glory came in the 1979 Cotton Bowl against Houston, when his team trailed 34-12 with 7:25 to play before Steve Cichy returned a blocked punt for a TD. Quarterback Joe Montana, suffering from hypothermia on a bitter cold day in Dallas where sleet had made the field like a skating rink, took over and displayed the same come-from-behind talent that has made him so successful in pro football. First, he passed for two points after

Above: Devine left Notre Dame after the 1980 season, but one of his biggest games that season was a come-from-behind late-game victory over Michigan, 29-27.

Opposite: Devine gets a ride on the shoulders of Scott Zettek (left) and Mike Shiner after a big 7-0 victory over Alabama in 1980.

Cichy's TD, then drove his team 61 yards in five plays, running two yards for a TD and again passing for two points as the Irish trailed 34-28 with 4:15 to play. Montana lost the ball on a fumble on his next possession, but when the Cougars decided to go on 4th-and-one at their 28-yard line, the Irish held. With 28 seconds to play, Montana drove for the victory, passing eight yards to Kris Haines on the final play. Joe Unis then kicked the winning point.

That victory was in the best tradition of Rockne, Leahy and Parseghian, but somehow it just wasn't the same under Devine, whose quirks had begun to wear thin with some of the school's inner circle. Two years later he won 10 of 11 games and, despite outplaying national champion Georgia in the Sugar Bowl, lost 17-14. Devine left after the season, still relatively unappreciated but satisfied that he had carried on the school's winning tradition, which is all anyone had a right to expect. But since the days of Rockne, whoever thought Notre Dame fans might have reasonable expectations?

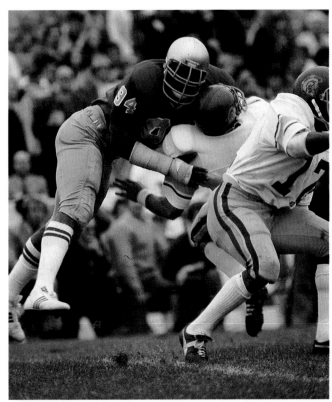

Left: *Devine's Irish buried Southern Cal 49-19 en route to the 1977 national title (left photo)* but Joe Montana *(right photo) had the greatest comeback win in the 1979 Cotton Bowl.*

GILMOUR DOBIE

Record:

North Dakota State (1906-07)	7-0-0
Washington (1908-16)	58-0-3
Navy (1917-19)	17-3-0
Cornell (1920-35)	82-36-7
Boston College (1936-38)	16-6-5

Below: *Gil Dobie is surrounded by his Cornell players in 1921. He won 26 consecutive games for the Big Red, and never once conceded that he might have a good team.*

Gil Dobie's 1925 team had just lost a heartbreaking game, 7-0, to Pennsylvania when his coaching friend, Pop Warner, dropped in to commiserate.

"I'm sorry you lost," Warner told him, "but it was a technical treat to see your backs get off their marks. I never saw quicker starters."

"That was the trouble," Dobie shot back.

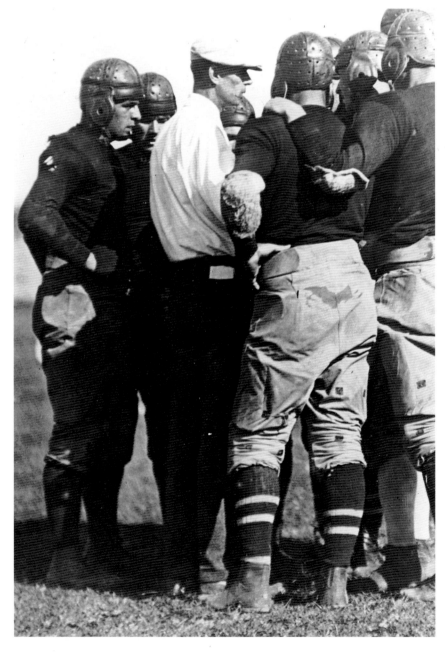

"They got to the tacklers too soon."

Three years later after Penn walloped Cornell 49-9, a Cornell alumnus met Dobie and said, "That was really sad, Mr. Dobie."

"Sad!" Dobie exclaimed. "Young man, you don't know what sorrow is. Wait till next year."

This was pure Gloomy Gil Dobie, the man who many believe wrote the book for all the prophet-of-doom talk which seems to be the native tongue for so many coaches. Often coaches use it to set up opponents, or get their team's attention. But Dobie really believed what he said.

Being a prophet of doom is one thing if a coach's teams are chronic losers, but Dobie's teams weren't. In fact, they didn't lose a game during his first dozen seasons. They weren't losers at North Dakota State; nor at Washington, where his teams were unbeaten for nine straight seasons and won 58 and tied three games; nor even at Navy where he suffered his first loss; nor during some great seasons at Cornell, where the Big Red ran off 26 straight wins; nor at his final stop at Boston College, where he once was so determined to finish a practice that he defied the warnings that preceded the Great Hurricane of 1938, until the wind swept him 30 feet across the field.

Dobie made abject pessimism part of his coaching bible. "It is harder to key a victorious team to the proper emotional pitch," he once wrote. "Even a few victories will make it a difficult problem for any coach. When you win consistently for years and victories become a common thing, how are you going to key your men?

"The only system I use is to talk to my players and try to convince them that there is danger ahead. Their fears must be aroused, and the coach himself must be conscientious in believing that danger is faced. Usually, he will be sincere if he is a wise coach. He knows that chance, luck, the breaks of the game are such large factors in football that it can easily reverse, checkmate and overpower every other advantage a team may enjoy.

"It is absolute ignorance of football that will lead a man to believe anything else. The overconfident player is not only a fool, he is actually ignorant of 50 percent of this game of football."

Dobie practiced what he preached. After one of his Washington teams defeated California 72-0, he made his players run laps around the stadium because they were playing the same team two weeks later and he wanted them to stay in the "proper frame of mind." It almost didn't work, because the Huskies had to rally in the fourth quarter to win 14-7. This just reinforced Dobie's convictions that no game ever is secure, no opponent is ever unbeatable.

He declared that he never coached players of All-America caliber, yet two great stars from his teams at Cornell, George Pfann and Eddie Kaw, are in the Hall of Fame. He was hostile toward the press and where most coaches at least try to keep peace with the faculty and alumni, he antagonized them at Cornell, claiming it was "nearly impossible to coach Phi Beta Kappas because they want to win by brain power, not muscle and emotional power, and that can't be done." Yet Pfann, one of Cornell's greatest players, was a Rhodes Scholar after he graduated from Cornell.

Dobie once suggested to the governing national collegiate sports body that players not be required to attend classes during the season. Naturally, he was castigated by those who believed he favored football over scholarship. He didn't, of course, but as often happened, he got too caught up in his fanatical belief that confidence meant defeat, and emotion keyed winning football. He tried to clarify the matter by declaring: "The only reason a boy comes to college is to study. If football interferes with his studies, he should drop football."

He was just as relentless in browbeating his players. At Washington, prior to a 1911 game against Idaho, one of his backs, Melvin Mucklestone, fell asleep and snored during his pre-game talk. Dobie screamed at the entire team, "I hope you get licked," and refused to say a word during the entire game. Of course, Washington won 17-10. He also once made a quarterback carry the ball for 12 consecutive plays because the young man had attended a fraternity dance and "stuffed his face with fudge" the night before the game. As the boy staggered off the field, sick to his stomach, Dobie gave him a further tongue-lashing.

Yet, away from the field, and after the football season, this lean man of Scottish descent was a charming companion in social situations, capable of enthralling small groups with his stories, and was always an insightful participant in conversations covering any variety of non-football topics. He

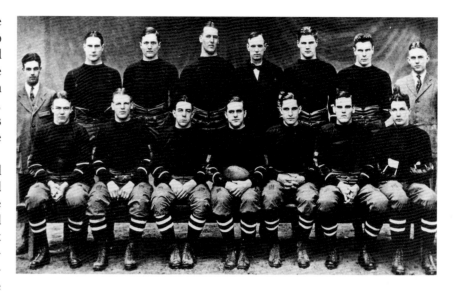

openly bragged that he "never took the game home" with him and was a dutiful family man, left to raise his two children from an early age following the tragic death of his young wife in an auto accident.

Despite all his coaching success, and the eventual riches he enjoyed from shrewd investments, his single great legacy is his absolute dependence upon the down side. Right or wrong, he built his game preparation philosophy around this darker side, even crying before a game. At Cornell, he often watched from a locker room window as his opponents warmed up and cried out to his players, "Look boys, they're big as pit bulls, and fast as jackrabbits. My God!"

Of course, Dobie's teams never lacked for size. Though he never weighed more than 150 pounds during his playing days at Minnesota, when he led the Gophers to their first Big Ten title in 1905, he had a passion for size and speed on his teams. He wanted players thick-thighed, big-calved, and heavy-ankled for power and drive. When, as a

Above: *Dobie's 1922 Cornell team won all eight of its games and featured two of the school's greatest players, George Pfann and Eddie Kaw (third and fourth from left, front row).*

Below: *Eddie Kaw, a Hall of Famer, was just one of several All-America players coached by Dobie. Here, he gains 10 yards around left end against Dartmouth as Cornell won, 50-7, in a 1921 game.*

Above: *Dobie never met a situation that gave him reason to live up to his nickname "Gloomy Gil." While at Boston College, he once tried to beat a hurricane by holding practice. Although he wasn't used to losing, he lost that battle, as he lost to Holy Cross 20-0 in this 1937 game.*

young assistant coach at Minnesota under Dr. Henry Williams, he was asked by a reporter how he sought players, Dobie's now-famous reply was: "When I'm travelling I ask farm boys how to get to a certain place. If they point with their finger, I move on. If they pick up the plow and point with it, I stop and sell them on the University of Minnesota."

He never was an innovator, but he was a relentless perfectionist. During the years when his teams steamrolled opponents, he was acclaimed as the greatest drill master in football and his teams exemplified an unsurpassed mechanical perfection. It was not unusual for him to spend an entire practice session teaching just one play, or to take two hours to school a center or guard in a blocking technique or a back in a foot move.

Dobie built his offense totally on the off-tackle play, but because he was such a great teacher, it was meticulously coached. Some claimed that his quarterbacks could have called the play out loud

and opponents still could not have stopped it. He had enough imagination to mix in some passing, but only after walking his quarterbacks down the field and showing them the areas where they could, and could not, throw the ball.

All of this was parlayed into fantastic success. At Washington, his teams never lost but attendance dwindled because fans found winning monotonous. No wonder Dobie worried about too much success!

His former players still chuckle about the times they were banished from the practice field or demoted to the second or third team after making a mistake, and told never to return. When they showed up the next day, they were accepted, usually with the comment, "I knew your pride wouldn't let you quit."

All of this only hardened his players' attitude that if they could take Dobie day after day, they could take anybody on Saturday afternoon. Most often they did.

BOBBY DODD

Record:

Georgia Tech (1945-66) 165-64-8

"In Dodd We Trust."

That was the motto that bound together the realm of Georgia Tech football for 22 years, when Robert Lee Dodd was head coach.

During that time, the Ramblin' Wreck went to more post-season games than any college team in the nation, when there were far fewer bowl games than there are now. This meant a team could only get to a bowl game the old-fashioned way – by earning the right.

Dodd's teams seemed to earn everything they achieved, but so did their head coach, though there were many who attributed much of his – and Georgia Tech's – success to a phenomenon called "Dodd's Luck." This always became a topic for discussion after Georgia Tech had come up with some amazing play, or after Dodd had junked conventional thinking and played according to his instincts, most often with excellent results.

"Lucky?" Dodd once said. "Bet your life I'm lucky. I'm lucky and so are my teams. It's a habit. You know, if you think you're lucky, you are."

Great coaches must be lucky to have big winning records, but they also must be smart and always ahead of the opposition, particularly if they do not have great talent year after year. This was the case with Dodd at Georgia Tech, whose teams always seemed to be too light, too slow, and too small. Frank Broyles, a great coach at Arkansas and later its athletic director, spent years as an assistant coach under Dodd, and he had another explanation. "I don't know how he did it, but some of the things Coach Dodd would pull made the players understand that he was a person with a mystique that went beyond the average man."

Dodd was a good, solid coach whose players loved to play for him because he tried to make the game fun. Dodd was also a meticulous planner, which he combined with a knack for being one step ahead of the opposition in the heat of a game. He often confounded his own coaches and players, as in the final game of the 1952 season when Georgia Tech was trying to finish a perfect season and gain a national championship. The Yellow Jackets trailed Georgia 10-7 in the third quarter and had the ball, 4th-and-four at Georgia's 10-yard line. Broyles was directing the offense, and Dodd told him that he wanted a belly pass with Chappell Rhino throwing the ball.

"Don't do it, coach," Broyles told his boss. "Rhino hasn't worked on that play in a year, and he

hasn't played 30 minutes this year."

Dodd ignored this advice, called Chappell over and described what the offense would do and how Georgia's defense would react, including how their end would tackle the fullback when the quarterback faked a belly play. "The quarterback will then pitch the ball to you and Buck Martin will be in the back of the end zone," Dodd told Rhino. "If the halfback comes up, throw it to Buck. If he doesn't, you can walk into the end zone."

The play worked just as Dodd had described, and Tech went on to win the game and the national title. "I couldn't watch because I thought we had blown the whole season," Broyles said. "But Bobby knew exactly what he was doing."

Basically, he did good solid coaching, which he had seen while playing quarterback for Gen. Bob Neyland at the University of Tennessee where he still is considered one of the greatest players in that school's history. Neyland had such unwavering

Above: *Bobby Dodd was one of the few coaches in football history who stayed at one school during his entire career. He led Georgia Tech to 165 victories during 22 seasons, and is the Ramblin' Wreck's winningest coach.*

Above: *Dodd won a national championship in 1952, and his team had an almost mystic belief in his ability to come up with the right play at the right time. Pepper Rodgers (second row, second from right) later became a successful coach.*

faith in Dodd's knowledge of the game that once, when a Georgia Tech scout missed most of a game between the Vols and the University of Kentucky, he was directed by Neyland to Dodd for a scouting report on both teams. The Tech assistant, Mack Tharpe, was so impressed with Dodd's summation that he pestered his own boss, Bill Alexander, into hiring him as an assistant.

Alexander was one of the lions of the game and Dodd became his chief assistant, staying for 14 years and resisting countless offers to coach elsewhere, before succeeding his boss. "Coach Alex was like a daddy to me," Dodd often said. "He thought of me as his son but he was a dominating person, and wanted to control me like a son. But he loved me and wouldn't let me leave Tech."

Unlike Alexander, Dodd was a highly imaginative coach and he was allowed to install an offense called "Hot Magic," in which the power of the single wing was transformed into a series of spinners and reverses, with a premium on deception and laterals that perplexed defenses. It was a key to Tech's first post-season win, in the 1939 Orange Bowl.

When Dodd finally became head coach in 1945, his "Hot Magic" suffered from a lack of playing talent as World War II had finally sapped Tech, and he suffered the first of just two losing seasons. Tech alumni grumbled mightily that perhaps the "fun-loving young coach" was overmatched. What they ignored was Dodd switching Tech to the T-formation and having to use Ed Holtsinger, a converted center, as his quarterback. He knew it would take a year for the change to produce results, and he would then have fine athletes again for his program.

He was correct because in 1946 and 1947, following 9-1 and 8-2 seasons, he won his first two post-season games, and when the 1950s rolled around,

his teams became a national power. His success included a 31-game winning streak from 1951 to 1953, and six straight bowl victories from 1951 to 1957. His teams thrived on the "belly play," which he picked up from quarterback Eddie LeBaron, a member of his College All-Star team, who had played at College of the Pacific under the immortal Amos Alonzo Stagg. The play demanded precision, because the quarterback rolled down the line of scrimmage, holding the ball in the belly of the fullback who ran along with him for a couple of steps. He either let the fullback keep the ball, or pulled it out and tossed it to a trailing halfback. Dodd also used the bootleg pass very effectively, once getting six straight completions in a devastating 42-19 victory over West Virginia in the 1955 Sugar Bowl.

But even outside his demand for precision in his offense, Dodd's coaching style was considered "unusual" by most standards. He laid the strategical groundwork in spring practice, did the heavy contact work in pre-season practice and then rarely scrimmaged his players during the season. His practices never lasted more than 90 minutes, and everything was geared to learning, and allowing his players to have "fun." This technique was deceiving to many opponents, such as LSU in 1946, who were amazed to see Tech players playing volleyball on the day before a game in Baton Rouge. They went to bed content that Dodd's team was a pigeon, and were stunned the next afternoon when they lost 26-7.

When Georgia Tech went to the Cotton Bowl in 1955, Dodd, as was always his custom in post-season games, wanted his players to have a good time, and he was lenient with them. Quarterback Wade Mitchell said the team returned to campus the day after Christmas and played volleyball for three days before leaving for Dallas, where it enjoyed several parties before playing Arkansas,

which Mitchell called "the meanest bunch of guys I ever saw."

"Our guys were 10 pounds overweight and seemed out of breath just walking from the locker room to our bench," Mitchell added. "Arkansas came out, lined up and ran three 100-yard sprints, and we're looking at them, and then at Coach Dodd and wondering, 'This guy did this to us?' Of course, we won the game 14-6."

"Nobody else can coach like Dodd and still win," Alabama coach Bear Bryant once grumbled.

This easy-going approach (though Dodd also disciplined when he had to, once dropping two starters from his team for rule infractions) and his continuing success led to the charges of "Dodd's Luck." But it wasn't all luck.

"Bobby just always seemed a thought ahead of the competition," former assistant Ray Graves said. "And when they played the 'Star Spangled Banner' and the game started, we felt we had the best coach on the sideline and believed we were always going to win the game."

Above: *Wade Mitchell was an All-America quarterback and co-captain of Dodd's 1952 national champions. He led the Ramblin' Wreck to victory over Arkansas in the Cotton Bowl to cap a perfect season.*

VINCE DOOLEY

Record:

Georgia (1964-88) 201-77-10

Below: *Vince Dooley was only the sixth Division 1-A coach ever to win more than 200 games. He had 201 victories for Georgia during a 25-season career that also included the 1980 national championship.*

The night of September 19, 1964 was not unlike any other late summer evening in Tuscaloosa, Alabama, the air heavy with the heat that had accumulated from another stifling summer and settled into the red clay soil around the huge stadium on the campus of the University of Alabama. On the field, the white-jerseyed visitors from the University of Georgia had come to play Bear Bryant's Alabama Crimson Tide, but more important in the lives of millions of Georgians was the unveiling of a new football coach: Vince Dooley.

Dooley had succeeded Johnny Griffith, who had served just three years after the legendary Wally Butts had retired, and the results had been less

than expected. Now Dooley, 32 years old and having had no head coaching experience save for a successful tour as freshman coach at his alma mater, Auburn University, was visibly nervous. But this was more from anticipation of at last digging his heels into a long-sought head coaching job than at the prospect of trying to succeed in an atmosphere where losing is not tolerated.

"I was absolutely convinced we were going to win the game," Dooley remembered years later. "I had planned everything to the finest detail and had it all written out. I didn't see any way we could lose."

Neither did Bryant and his quarterback, Joe Namath, as they began a journey toward a national championship with a rousing 31-3 victory that night.

A year later, the two met again on another hot, late summer afternoon, at Sanford Stadium in Athens, Georgia. This time Dooley was no rookie coach, and his Bulldogs handed Alabama its only loss of that season, 18-17. Bryant could only smile

Left: *Running back Herschel Walker broke all kinds of records as a freshman in 1980 and led Georgia Tech to the national championship that season.*

and shake the hand of the newest bright, young coach on the block.

Nearly a quarter-century later, after he had been at one school longer than any active coach at the time – he retired as Georgia's head coach following the 1988 season – Dooley acknowledged that he may have been the last of a breed of football coach that had made the sport King of Dixie. This breed began with Bill Alexander and Dan McGugin, in the early years of the century, and continued through such great coaching stalwarts as Wallace Wade, Gen. Robert R. Neyland, Wally Butts, Frank Howard, Bobby Dodd, Shug Jordan, Johnny

Vaught and Bear Bryant – men who ruled football empires for decades with singular success.

Dooley certainly had as much success – and in some cases, more – than those coaching legends. In the end, he also became a coaching legend in the state of Georgia, having equalled the feats of both Butts and Dodd, but having done it quietly – so quietly that it came as a great shock to many that he was ready to retire after a quarter-century on the job, and that he had accumulated over 200 victories, only the sixth coach in Division 1-A history to reach that magical figure. In fact, his 201 victories produced a national championship in 1980,

Right: *Dooley was never flamboyant in either his personal style or his football. He believed in rushing the football if at all possible, an attack which was keyed by Heisman Trophy winner Herschel Walker.*

six Southeastern Conference titles and 20 trips to post-season games. Only Bryant, among all other SEC coaches, won more titles and games.

"I remember when people were calling me the first of the young guard," Dooley said. "I remember going against people like Bryant and Dodd, thinking I could just outwork them. I never could, because I soon learned that you never got to be an old coach if you don't know how to work."

Dooley certainly knew how to work, but he never was splashy; if anything, he was almost too plain in the way he went about his job. He spoke in a soft monotone, never trying to inspire with the sound of his voice as Bryant did with his growl, or Butts with his thick drawl. His teams were also un-

dramatic: efficient on both offense and defense, with a greater leaning to the running game than to the risky passing attack. He relied heavily on solid defense to produce scoring opportunities; and indeed, during his national championship season in 1980, that unit got more notoriety than the offense, which featured running back Herschel Walker.

Walker keyed Dooley's Golden Era – from 1980 through 1983 – when his teams won 43 games, lost only four and tied one, and made four straight major bowl trips, three of them to the Sugar Bowl, with national championships on the line each time. Walker, a six-foot, two-inch, 220-pounder, started this string of successes by smashing all existing records for freshman running backs in 1980 by gaining over 1600 yards in 11 games. The Dawg Defense, an opportunistic band coached by the smooth-domed Erk Russell (whose players also sported shiny pates), led the country in turnovers and played a key role in Dooley's crowning achievement – a 17-10 victory over Notre Dame in the Sugar Bowl that clinched an unbeaten season and Georgia's first national championship.

The following season, with Walker gaining 1891 yards, Georgia lost only to eventual national champion Clemson before losing to Pitt in another Sugar Bowl appearance, and spoiling any chance for a second straight title. In 1982, Walker had 1752 yards rushing for unbeaten Georgia, which played Penn State in the Sugar Bowl for the national championship. The teams were ranked 1-2 but Penn State jumped out to a 20-3 lead in the second quarter and held on to win 27-23.

Dooley got his prized 200th victory in the final game of his final season, an emotional 24-3 victory over rival Georgia Tech, and then won the final game of his career, 34-27 over Michigan State in a most un-Dooley-like fashion – his team threw the ball 27 times and scored twice on TD passes.

At the end, his team carried him off the field on their shoulders, and into the halls of memories where his feats rightfully joined with those of Bryant, Wade, Neyland, Dodd, Butts and Vaught.

Below: Dooley gets a ride off the Gator Bowl gridiron after his team's 34-27 victory over Michigan State in 1988, for the final win of his career.

HAYDEN FRY

Record:

So. Methodist (1962-72)	49-66-1
North Texas (1973-78)	40-23-3
Iowa (1979-89)	82-46-4*

*Still active

"Calling Dr. Fry. Calling Dr. Fry."

Hayden Fry has answered that call for most of his coaching life when moribund football programs needed resuscitating and, like a skilled football physician, he has brought them back to health.

Fry has been at this business for over a quarter of a century, and he became so skilled that going into the 1990s, he ranks Number 5 in victories among all active Division 1-A coaches. He has been chosen as Coach of the Year in three conferences – Southwest, Missouri Valley and Big Ten.

The life of a football program resuscitator is totally different from that of coaches who enjoy long and fruitful reigns at one school for most of their careers and build up great individual recognition and continuity. A coach like Fry may take several seasons to turn poor programs around, and like the old western sheriff who rids the town of the bad guys, he often feels compelled to move on and find another town to clean up.

There is no single "right way" to put an ailing team back on its feet, and in Fry's case, he uses his own unique philosophy of "scratch it where it itches," which means he takes what he has and uses it to his best advantage. When he took over as head coach at Southern Methodist University in 1961, where the program had produced only two victories and a tie in two seasons, it took him five years before he produced a winner. Part of his solution was a pioneering effort – signing the first black player in the history of the Southwest Conference, a marvelous wide receiver named Jerry Levias.

When he went to North Texas State University

Right: *Hayden Fry, who has resuscitated three moribund football programs during his career, isn't afraid to venture into losing territory and come out with bowl bids and conference titles.*

in 1973, which had won only seven games in the previous four seasons, his final four seasons were winning ones, but he got discouraged and left when that success could not bring post-season invitations to bowl games.

Iowa was a different matter – a graveyard of coaches yearning to become alive with success. The Hawkeyes had won just 29 games in the previous 10 years, and ran their streak to 19 consecutive non-winning seasons until Fry guided them to the Rose Bowl after the 1981 season.

"I wouldn't have come to Iowa had I not believed we could win," Fry said. "I'd been offered a lot of jobs over the years, and each had to be judged on its own merit."

Some questioned his judgment when he took on a job where four previous coaches had failed. But Fry had been through it all before, and he needed only the nod from former coaches Forest Evashevski and Jerry Burns. Evashevski had led Iowa to its last great moments of glory in the late 1950s, and Burns had been their last winning coach, in 1961. Both told Fry he could succeed.

"At first," Fry said, "I wasn't sure that Iowa knew how to win, so I had to change all that."

Like any physician trying desperately to save the patient, Fry took unusual measures. First, he got the Super Bowl champion Pittsburgh Steelers to

Above: *Fry's 1981 Hawkeye team stunned the Big Ten by winning a share of the conference title and a berth in the Rose Bowl. He deftly mixed a good passing game with the conference's traditional reliance on running to win some big games.*

Left: *Chuck Long was an All-America quarterback for Fry at Iowa during the 1980s and helped make Fry the winningest coach in the Hawkeyes' history.*

Above: Fry's hallmark as a coach is his demand that his players give an all-out performance, as Larry Station is doing here against Michigan. "I have no secrets for success," Fry says. "I work hard and I expect my players to do the same. Then, we should win."

send him one of their uniforms, which were the same black and gold colors as Iowa. "They sent me Terry Bradshaw's uniform, which couldn't have been better since he was the ultimate winner in everyone's mind, "Fry said. "I modeled our uniforms after the Steelers, at least giving us the look of a winner."

Then he got a new football complex constructed, and worked round the clock with his coaches and players to rid the program of the negativism that had been plaguing it for years. Iowa's players learned that Fry demanded 60 minutes of effort in every game, and that began with two hours of total effort in every practice. Fry startled many in his first season, 1979, with a 5-6 record that included four victories in the Big Ten. But Fry warned Hawkeye fans that his second season often was one of his poorest – 4-7 at SMU and 2-7-2 at North Texas – and this time was no different, as Iowa won only four of 11 games, though three of those losses were by a total of 11 points.

Hardly anyone was expecting much improvement in 1981, but during the losses of 1980, his team began to energize itself with consistent play, and with players Fry had brought into the system who were able to handle his wide-open offense, something that he had learned growing up in Texas and playing in the pass-happy Southwest Con-

ference (at Baylor) in the late 1940s.

He shocked everyone when his 1981 team tied Ohio State for the Big Ten crown, and included among its victories that season were upsets over Nebraska, the Big Eight champion, and Michigan. His biggest victory that season was beating Purdue for the first time since 1960, assuring Iowa of its first winning season since 1961.

"Once we got that monkey off our backs, we seemed to relax," Fry said, "and from then on, success at Iowa was not a one-time thing."

This time, the sheriff who cleaned up the town decided to stay and enjoy the fruits of his labor. Hawkeye fans love it, because almost all home games have been sellouts, thanks to an offense that has compiled the top pass efficiency rating in college football for six straight seasons. His teams are well-rounded, having led the Big Ten in total defense in three of those years, and placed in the top three in the Big Ten six times in an eight-season span.

His 82 victories through the 1989 season have made him the winningest coach in Iowa history, and his teams have won more games under his direction than Iowa teams turned in during the previous 21 seasons. Included in that success are a pair of Big Ten titles and eight consecutive post-season games.

JAKE GAITHER

Record:

Florida A&M (1945-69)   203-36-4

During his quarter century as head coach at Florida A&M, Alonzo "Jake" Gaither had so many talented players that his team could often score at will – and it did. His motto was: "Ask no quarter, give no quarter – kill a mosquito with an ax!" Only once in his 25 seasons as head coach of the Rattlers did he ever lose as many as four games in one season, and twice he lost only three games. The rest of the time he lost only one or two games – except for the three seasons that his teams were unbeaten. "I can teach a lot more character by winning than I can by losing," he said. Gaither was always determined to succeed in his way, regardless of the situation, both on and off the gridiron. When he wanted to add a couple of rooms to his home in Tallahassee, Florida, but at the expense of an old pine tree that his wife Sadie loved, she told him: "If you want the rooms, you'll have to build them around that pine tree." So he did – and they are probably the only rooms in America that have a huge, live pine tree as a centerpiece.

Gaither was much more than a football coach to the thousands of students with whom he came in contact, and that is his greatest legacy at this once all-black school in Florida's northwest panhandle. Johnnie Williams, one of the school's assistant football coaches who also had played for Gaither, once said that his coach "was the main male figure in my life."

"He came to Louisville and brought me to Florida A&M. He looked after me for five years when I was a player. He was influential in my obtaining all the jobs I got. He gave me advice throughout. I was raised without a father and sometimes I wonder what it would have been like to have had a father. Jake has filled a whole lot of that . . . Just a person who's been there. Fair, a friend – just, I guess, a great daddy."

"It wasn't just players," noted Ken Riley, one of Gaither's great players and a great defensive back for the NFL's Cincinnati Bengals, who later became head coach of the Rattlers. "It was the student body in general. Everybody called him Poppa Gaither."

When new employees were hired by the school while Gaither was head coach, they had their priorities – and the first was finding his office. "One of the greatest honors I had was to be president during his time," noted Dr. B.L. Perry. "He was the biggest thing we had. He was in Bear Bryant's class."

In fact he beat Bryant to the 200-victory mark, becoming only the fourth coach at the Division I level (there were no 1-A and 1-AA distinctions then) ever to win more than 200 games – Amos Alonzo Stagg, Bob Zuppke and Jess Neely of Rice had already reached that plateau when Gaither won his 200th game, 10-7 over Southern University, in his last season, 1969.

Though the school was an all-black institution for all of his career, its football program was as up-to-date as any at the Southeastern Conference or Big Ten level.

"I'll stack my coaching up against anybody's," he said. "We never stopped learning. For 25 years, we ran a clinic. We had integrated coaching clinics long before integration came. I had Bear Bryant come down; also Bobby Dodd from Georgia Tech, Frank Broyles from Arkansas, Woody Hayes from Ohio State. We had outstanding coaching at Florida A&M."

Below: *Jake Gaither was more than a football coach to his players, many of whom were raised without fathers. He influenced them off the field and steered them into successful positions after their college lives were finished.*

Right: *Gaither's most famous player was Bob Hayes, who also won a pair of gold medals in the 1964 Olympics and later was the most feared pass receiver in the NFL when he played for the Dallas Cowboys.*

That resulted in outstanding results, as well. His teams had a .849 winning percentage, topped only by Notre Dame's Knute Rockne and Frank Leahy in Division I annals. He also won six black national championships, and won the Southern Intercollegiate Athletic Conference championship 22 of the 25 years he coached. He produced at least one All-America player every year, and in all, 35 players were named to the various All-A teams. Forty-two of his players played professional football, including running back Willie Galimore with the Chicago Bears and Bob Hayes, who also was a great back at Florida A&M but an All-Pro wide receiver with the Dallas Cowboys. Hayes also won the gold medal in the 100-meter run – "the world's fastest human" designation – at the 1964 Olympic Games in Tokyo.

Gaither didn't intend to become a football coach until his father, who was a minister in Dayton, Tennessee, died when Jake was a senior at Knoxville College. His father wanted him to follow in his steps, and Jake had visions of becoming a great lawyer, spending much of his spare time at the local courthouse listening to lawyers plead their cases.

The death of his father made him the chief provider for his family, and the quickest available job was as a high school teacher and coach. He worked at that level for the next 12 years (while also earning his master's degree in health and physical education at Ohio State during a half-dozen summers) before joining William Bell's staff in 1937. He succeeded Herman Nelson as head coach in 1945, and he was on the hot seat from the beginning because the Rattlers had a record of football excellence since beginning the sport on an organized basis in 1933. (The school has won 75 percent of its games through the 1989 season.)

Gaither won because he was a motivator and a perfectionist – and because the well-coached players he sent back into Florida's high school coaching ranks provided him a "feeder" system with players who had the "Gaither touch."

He was demonstrative on the practice field, raising his voice when it was needed, but never relying on profanity to make his points. He got down on the ground, when necessary, to teach techniques, and then he demanded that his players be precise and spirited whenever they played. On game days, some of his locker room talks were legendary – a combination of the preacher his father wished him to be, and the lawyer-pleading-his-case that he had once envisioned. It also helped that segregation was in vogue in the South during his tenure and the white Southern schools refused to recruit black players, leaving them to such schools as Florida A&M.

Gaither was a force unto himself. When his team's bus once was stopped in Alabama for a minor traffic violation, Gaither seethed. He then called the governor of Florida and very quickly, the Rattlers were on their way – with a police escort.

When his team was upset by rival Tennessee State in 1967, he promised: "Somebody's going to pay." Those "somebody's" were his players during the following week's practice sessions, and Central State of Ohio the next Saturday by the score of 54-0.

The one game that stands out in his mind was a 34-28 victory over the University of Tampa in 1969. It was the first interracial game his team had ever played.

"It really wasn't important that we won the game," he said. "What was important was I had felt we were ready for an interracial game, and the Board of Regents had finally agreed after turning it down several times.

"Coach (Fran) Curci felt the same way, so we agreed to play," he continued. "The Regents felt there might be some tension before, during and after the game around Tallahassee. But I felt I could control the Negro fans and Coach Curci felt the whites would cause no trouble.

"So, when we prepared for the game, both of us emphasized that it was no different than any other game. And you know what? There was not a single incident. Not before, during or after the game. Everything was great."

Gaither's pet nickname for his players was "baby" but it was never used in the "hipster" sense, but as a term of endearment. Some say that it had a two-pronged meaning – one to compliment, as in "you've been a good baby," and the other to chastise, as in "Baby, why did you do that?" Gaither says the term is simply one of endearment. "I never wanted them to feel I was so far above them," he said. "I thought of them as being very close to me."

They always were, and still are, and exalted with him back in 1975 when he received college football's "triple crown" of awards – the Amos Alonzo Stagg Award from the American Football Coaches Association, its highest honor; the Walter Camp Award, given for football contributions and humanitarian honors; and his election to the National Football Foundation Hall of Fame.

In 1978, the Alonzo Smith "Jake" Gaither Trophy was established, and it is considered the black college football counterpart to the Heisman Trophy. Everyone who wins it must know that he had earned the honor – Jake Gaither would have it no other way.

Left: *Gaither won the small college division coach of the year honor in 1961 while his friend, Bear Bryant (left), was major college recipient. Gaither was the fourth coach in college football history to win 200 games, and beat Bryant to that mark.*

WOODY HAYES

Record:

Denison (1946-48)	19-6-0
Miami (Ohio) (1949-50)	14-5-0
Ohio State (1951-79)	205-61-10

The true measure of any coach's success is how his players feel about him at least a decade after they have finished playing for him.

There is no public record that anyone coached by Wayne Woodrow "Woody" Hayes, and away from his day-to-day influence for even five years, ever bad-mouthed him. This, of course, flies in the face of a common perception that Hayes was some kind of madman, who intimidated, browbeat and otherwise treated those under his command in a sub-human manner. The truth of the matter is that he sometimes did browbeat and intimidate his players, but he also taught them, wetnursed them,

inspired them and in general, regardless of manner or means, often lifted them to a higher plane of accomplishment both on and off the playing field.

Hayes was single-minded and often stubborn to a fault during his great coaching career, but he was no different from any of the great coaches who gained their greatest strengths from their strong beliefs and refusal to be moved from them. He was often ridiculed for his "three yards and a cloud of dust" offenses, which were conceived in a day when that was the accepted style, and for his alleged refusal to open up his offenses to more passing because, he once said, "three things happen when you pass, and two of them are bad." Yet, because he deviated from his strongest principle only when he had the tools to make the change successful, no teams ever did a better job of mixing runs and passes than his two national championship teams in 1954 and 1968.

His stubbornness is just one reason why Hayes, with 238 victories (205 at Ohio State) is Number 4 on the all-time list of winningest Division 1-A coaches, and why in addition to three national

Right: *Woody Hayes' kingdom was the football field and Ohio State's magnificent practice facility now abuts Woody Hayes Drive. He also was a frequent university lecturer on military history, his other great interest.*

Left: *No one ever doubted who was boss when Hayes was around his football team, yet he had as much interest in his players' personal well-being as he did in the way they played football.*

Below: *Woody Hayes won a national championship with his 1968 team, one of three that he captured during his 29 seasons as head coach of the Buckeyes. He finished his career as Number 4 on the all-time victory list of major college coaches.*

Opposite top: *Hayes always stressed the positive with his players and each week before their final heavy practice, he told them how they were going to beat their upcoming opponent.*

Opposite bottom: *Hayes' offense was always called "three yards and a cloud of dust" because he loved to run the football. No one did it better for him than Archie Griffin (44), the only player ever to win two Heisman trophies.*

Above: *Hayes was known for his gruelling practices and his relentless perfectionism.*

titles, his Ohio State teams won seven Big Ten titles and shared six others.

The basis for this success was totally rooted in the way he coached football, and few ever did it more colorfully – or thoroughly. For example, his teams annually were the least penalized teams in the Big Ten, because Hayes insisted on strong discipline on the field, and because he used three officials every day in practice, who called penalties. The accused then had to face his coach – and that in itself was enough to cure bad habits. He filmed every practice so the coaching staff could be certain their game plans were precise. He repeated the same play time and time again in practice until he decided it was perfect, noting that all players don't learn at the same rate of speed, or with the same degree of mastery. "We don't change a player because he makes a mistake in practice," he said. "He may require more time to learn." No fundamental was overlooked – even the kicking game, to which he allotted at least 20 minutes every day.

He was a keen student of military history and spiced his football teaching with military parallels. One year, the November weather in Columbus lurked near the zero mark and OSU officials wanted him to practice indoors. But Hayes, the military historian, pointed out that during World War II, the Navy "was getting the hell kicked out of it in the North Atlantic because they were trained in the sunny Caribbean and couldn't fight in cold weather. When the Navy switched maneuvers to the North Atlantic, we got tougher and started winning. From now on, this team practices in the North Atlantic, no matter how cold it gets."

"We almost died," noted tackle Dave Foley, "but Woody did it for us, not for him, and we were better for it."

Hayes found many ways to make his players better, but he also inspired them in the process. Each week he awarded Buckeye decals, to be pasted on the back of a player's helmet, for exemplary play in the previous game. They became prized possessions. On Thursday before a game, Hayes met with his players before their last full practice, and typically, he told his players that they would win on Saturday because their opponents would respect them for being Ohio State, "and that respect soon turns to fear, and by the time we've hit them three or four times in that first quarter they know they can't win."

He held a full professorship at Ohio State, taught a class in football and often lectured in military history. He also insisted on classroom achievement, once pursuing a player to Massachusetts after he had left school and demanding that he return. "I don't care if you play football, but you must finish your education." The boy did both. When players went into pro football without receiving their degrees, he kept after them until they did.

Right: *Hayes ruled the sidelines with an iron hand, and he never hesitated to vent his feelings if he felt his team was not given a proper hearing of the rules. Yet, he also was cool and calculating in pressure situations, which accounted for many victories.*

Hayes never changed his lifestyle. He never made more than $40,000 a year from Ohio State, even when other coaches, some of far less achievement or skill, were making four and five times as much. He always kept his telephone number listed, and he was called countless times, often in the middle of the night, by irate fans. "If you make yourself available and sort of roll with the punch, the cranks will tire of it, and stop bothering you," he explained. For those who chose to hate him, the warning was, "Only until you hear him speak – and then you'll love him."

Hayes' kindness was as legendary as his irascibility. In he middle of one night, a player's family called to tell him the lad's sister was dying. Hayes got up, drove to the boy's dorm to break the news, then gave his car to the player's roommate and told him to drive the player home and stay as long as necessary. He then walked two miles back to his own home. On a cold day when the Buckeyes played at Iowa, Hayes sneaked behind the Hawkeyes bench and stole a couple of heaters for his own players. After a victory over Michigan that climaxed an unbeaten season, he kept President Richard M. Nixon waiting on a congratulatory phone call until he finished talking to his players.

Still, Hayes was an enigma to his players. He would cuff a boy on the helmet, or pop him in the

Left: *Hayes got 16 rides atop his players' shoulders after victories over arch-rival Michigan. Here, he is carried off after a 50-14 victory in 1968 that clinched the Big Ten title and a trip to the Rose Bowl, where his team beat Southern Cal and won the national title.*

stomach when he got exasperated with his repeated mistakes, and the player would go out and play better. His tirades at practice were measured by megatons, and by the number of coaching caps that were torn asunder until one day, no matter how hard he tried, a cap remained intact. He suddenly realized that his equipment man had overstitched every seam with extra-tough nylon thread, so he put it on his head, didn't acknowledge what had happened, and never destroyed another.

In a game against Michigan in 1971, an official missed an obvious interference call that prevented the Buckeyes from getting a chance for the winning points. Hayes berated the official and was penalized 15 yards. He then bent a yard marker over his knee, threw it onto the field, and ripped a flag off a downs marker and tore it to shreds. At other times, he knocked cameras from photographers who interrupted the sanctity of his sideline huddle, and once pushed a writer from his locker room after a loss when the man was slow to respond to Hayes' demands to leave. He even gave up coaching in high school when, after a losing season in 1940, his temper boiled over in a disagreement with his superiors and he joined the Navy, where he rose to the rank of lieutenant commander.

His most infamous temper tantrum cost him his job. During the Gator Bowl against Clemson in

Above: *Hayes' sideline tantrums were renowned, many of them the result of extremely high blood pressure that caused him to act irrationally, as happened when he struck this Clemson player during the 1979 Gator Bowl, for which he was subsequently fired.*

1979, he struck an opposing player after the boy had intercepted a pass and was downed near the Ohio State bench. Unknown to most people, Hayes was suffering from serious high blood pressure which sometimes reached such levels, as happened in this case, that he was unaware of his outbursts. However, this was the last straw for his superiors and after he refused their request that he resign, they fired him.

But during his career he had given Ohio State some great moments, after a shaky start in which he fought off demands for his scalp. In 1954, led by Heisman Trophy winner Hopalong Cassady, the Buckeyes won their first national championship in 12 years and then demolished Southern Cal 20-7 in the Rose Bowl. His sophomore-dominated 1968 team went undefeated and, for the first time that the two top-ranked teams ever met in a Rose

Bowl, the Buckeyes defeated USC and O. J. Simpson 24-10 and were voted Team of the Decade.

Hayes always said his "topper" came in the 1974 Rose Bowl. Ohio State and Michigan tied for the Big Ten title, but the conference voted to send the Buckeyes to play Southern Cal, which had humiliated Ohio State 42-17 the previous year. Hayes, the coach who hated to pass, set up three TDs by Pete Johnson with a crafty aerial game from Cornelius Greene, who also scored the fourth TD, and a TD reception by two-time Heisman Trophy winner Archie Griffin in a 42-21 victory. Shortly after the game, the USC president invited Hayes to lecture at the school on World War I.

"Thank you, sir," Hayes replied, "but I'd rather lecture on World War II. That war was not a stalemate."

Woody Hayes couldn't stand "stalemates."

JOHN WILLIAM HEISMAN

Record:

Oberlin (1892)	7-0-0
Akron (1893)	5-2-0
Oberlin (1894)	4-3-1
Auburn (1895-99)	12-4-2
Clemson (1900-03)	19-3-2
Georgia Tech (1904-19)	100-29-6
Pennsylvania (1920-22)	16-10-2
Washington & Jefferson (1923)	7-1-1
Rice (1924-27)	14-18-3

The Heisman Trophy, given each year to a college football player voted best in the country by the nation's sports media, is the game's most prestigious award. John William Heisman died in 1936 not even knowing his name would be forever attached to this coveted trophy. But long before a sculptor posed a football player from New York University and constructed the memento, Heisman's innovations had made the game of football worth watching, and more fun to play.

Consider that from his imagination came the following: the center snap; the verbal "hike" signal to center the ball; the division of the game into quarters; the scoreboard showing down, distance, time, and score; the movement of lighter offensive players to defensive positions where they were not overmatched; the spearheading of legislation to legalize the forward pass. Heisman developed these innovations while coaching at nine schools, having his greatest success at Georgia Tech where he won 100 games, including one victory by the biggest score in the game's history – 222-0 over Cumberland.

He coached in an era when his peers were such lions of the game as Amos Alonzo Stagg, Dr. Henry Williams, Pop Warner, Bob Zuppke, Percy Haughton, Fielding Yost and Knute Rockne. Each of these men had his own distinctive flair, and Heisman's was honed by his other true passion, Shakespearean acting. Everything he did was in a grand manner. His speech was flowery and perfectly intoned, and it rolled and tumbled as if the Olde Bard himself had been his personal tutor. He talked to his team in the most exaggerated stage English. "Thrust your projections into their cavities, grasping them about the knees and depriving them of their means of propulsion," he intoned on the art of tackling. His pre-game and halftime talks were equally as dramatic and richly delivered, as if the locker room was the stage.

Heisman played at Brown and Penn, and began coaching in the nineteenth century when football fields had no stripes at five-yard intervals; no linesmen and linesticks; the referee kept track of distance by dropping a handkerchief where he guessed the ball was last put into play; the game was played in 45-minute halves, not 15-minute quarters; players only had the hair on their heads for protection, which they would let grow from June 1 until the season ended; and most teams played twice a week.

True to his Shakespearean style, Heisman arrived at Clemson in 1900 in grand fashion – in pursuit of a young widow with whom he had become enamored, and whom he later married. Georgia Tech wooed him away from Clemson after losing to them 44-5 and 73-0 in successive years, by offering him the astronomical salary of $2000 to become the school's first full-time head coach. He left Atlanta in almost as dramatic fashion, summoning school officials to his home and announcing that he and his wife were divorcing. In parting amicably, he told his stunned superiors, he would allow her to make the first choice of where she wished to live, and he would seek a different locale. She chose Atlanta, so Heisman left to coach at Penn in 1920.

He introduced the famed Heisman Shift in 1910, one of the most feared offenses of that time. Rules of that time allowed guards and tackles to shift or line up in the backfield without coming to a stop

Below: *John Heisman was the first great coach in the South. His Georgia Tech team of 1916 ran up the biggest score in college football history, 222-0 over Cumberland.*

Above: *Heisman coached at nine schools during his career, and is pictured here with his 1922 Penn team. Yet he is best known for having the Heisman Trophy named in his honor after serving as sports director of New York City's Downtown Athletic Club.*

before the ball was snapped. Heisman's offense often had every player except the center behind the line of scrimmage; just how far behind depended on where the play was going.

"I pull my guards and tackles back to form the first line of interference. The halfbacks and ends form the second line. The moment the ball is passed (snapped), the two lines of interference move forward with all possible speed, and when, in a concerted formation it hits a straggling enemy line, the opposing defense line is knocked down. For end runs, fake kicks, forward passes or trick plays, the double line of interference forms a good mask."

This was his primary offense during his 16 years as Tech's head coach, when he reached his pinnacle as a coach and national figure. His teams were called the Golden Tornados, a forerunner of Tech's Yellow Jackets nickname, and a tornado they were. They rang up 35 games without a loss from 1914 to 1918, during which they outscored opponents 1599 to 67. Tech scored 105 points against Mercer in 1914, and got its record-setting 222 against Cumberland in 1915.

That game was played because although Cumberland hadn't fielded a team that year, it didn't want to lose a $3000 forfeiture bond it had posted the previous year. So 15 students volunteered to

said in a kindly manner.

"I'm on the right bench, sir," the boy replied just as kindly. "If I go to the other side of the field, they might send me back into the game."

Heisman allowed him to stay.

Heisman was as renowned for running up scores against hapless opponents as he was for his innovations and kooky training rules. He didn't allow his players to use soap or water during the week because he felt it was debilitating, and he forbade them to eat foods which he disliked. While the merit of such rules is debatable, no one can dispute the fertility of the mind that gave birth to so many innovations. For example, while scouting a game between Clemson and Georgia, he watched a harried Georgia punter fling a ball in desperation lest his kick be blocked, to a teammate who caught it and ran for a touchdown. Though it was clearly against the rules, the referee allowed it and Heisman saw the pass as a valid way to open up the game and relieve the terrible physical beatings players were taking in defensing the popular "flying wedge" offense.

He waited five years before proposing the change to legalize the forward pass to Walter Camp, then a one-man imprimatur of football rules, and another six years passed before he gathered enough support to have it declared legal, in 1906. He used it with great success, and then perfected the use of blockers to lead an end run. He loved quick, light players and armed them with a variety of trick, or "gadget," plays to take advantage of these physical attributes.

One of those "gadgets" was the "hidden ball" play, which came about during a talk with some of his players at Auburn in 1895. Noting that a youngster had once asked him if such a maneuver was legal, he opined that it was, but didn't know how to perform it. One of his players suggested hiding the ball beneath his jersey. Heisman yelled in delight, and drew up a play whereby a back pretended to take the center's snap and run with a full blocking convoy while the center – who had stuffed the ball under his jersey – lay prone until the crowd cleared. Then he got up and ran. The play soon became part of football's offense at that time.

After finishing his coaching tours at Penn and Rice, Heisman moved to New York City, where he became the athletic director of the Downtown Athletic Club. In a move to raise its stature, the club decided to award a trophy to the nation's outstanding college football player based on votes from sportswriters. The University of Chicago's Jay Berwanger won the first award, the D.A.C. Trophy, but when Heisman died early the following year, the award was renamed in his honor.

He never knew of it, but if he did, he surely would have had something rather Shakespearean to say.

play, and with such a mismatch, Tech scored 18 touchdowns in the first half for a 126-0 lead, and then agreed to shorten the second half. Incredibly, neither team made a first down because Georgia Tech scored on every play and Cumberland lost 10 fumbles. Sometimes, the game reached comical proportions, such as when Cumberland's quarterback, Eddie Edwards, fumbled the snap, and yelled for his teammates to pick up the ball.

"Pick it up yourself, you dropped it," a teammate yelled back.

Late in the game, Heisman discovered a Cumberland player hiding on his team's bench.

"You're on the wrong bench, son," Heisman

LOU HOLTZ

Record:

William & Mary (1969-71)	13-20-0
No. Carolina St. (1972-75)	33-12-3
Arkansas (1977-83)	60-21-2
Minnesota (1984-85)	10-12-0
Notre Dame (1986-89)	36-11-0*

*Still active

In 21 seasons, from 1969 to 1989, Lou Holtz has coached at five schools, and his list of accomplishments is truly impressive.

At William & Mary, despite three losing seasons, he took the school to its first post-season game after winning the Southern Conference championship in 1970.

At North Carolina State, Holtz produced the best four-season (1972-75) record (33-12-3) in the school's history after taking over a program that had won only three games in each of the three previous seasons. For the first time ever, the Wolfpack appeared in four consecutive post-season games, from 1972 to 1975; and in 1974, finished the season with a Number 9 ranking, also the first time in its history that it ever broke into the final top 10 ratings. The Wolfpack finished in the top 20 the other three seasons.

At Arkansas, Holtz succeeded the great Frank Broyles as coach, and bettered his record by becoming the first coach ever to average nine victories in each of his seven seasons (1977-83). This also was the first time that the school ever went to a post-season game for six straight years.

Holtz then went to Minnesota, where the Golden Gophers had been 1-10 the season before and had lost 17 straight conference games. In his second of two years as head coach, the team enjoyed its first winning season in five years, and made its first bowl appearance in eight seasons.

In Holtz's third season at Notre Dame, 1988, the

Right: *Lou Holtz's intense coaching style has served him well since 1969. In his third season as head coach at Notre Dame, he brought the Fighting Irish their first national championship in 12 years.*

Irish won the national championship, their first since 1977, and had an undefeated season, their first since 1973. In 1989, the Irish were 11-1, including a victory over top-ranked and undefeated Colorado in the Orange Bowl. Only a loss to national champion Miami cost them a second straight perfect season and national title.

That's a lot of work for a relatively short coaching career, but Holtz never minded hard work, just as he never minded the benefits which accrue from it, or the chance to move on and work his magic in some other football stadium. "Working magic" is no slip of the lip, because in addition to being a top football coach, Holtz also indulges in some sleight-of-hand for the enjoyment and amusement of friends and associates; and he is a much sought-after motivational speaker, who can give a pep talk that would enthrall Knute Rockne.

Holtz runs a gamut of emotions in his work. He is a stern disciplinarian and organizer who also has endured recalcitrant players for almost an entire season before cutting them loose on the eve of a big game, or before playing in a major bowl game. During a game, he ceaselessly paces a 20-yard section in front of his bench, hair askew, goggle-eyed behind thick glasses and looking like a man being torn asunder from within his five-foot, nine-inch frame by the events which are occurring on the playing field, even if his team is ahead by three touchdowns. Twenty minutes after a game ends, if his team has won, he can be a master quipster who charms the media and alumni about the events which just racked his spirit as if all that had transpired was a mere walk in the park.

At other times, he is a curious blend, a man with distinctive public and private personalities, a

driven, relentless, demanding person who has enough con man in him, and enough humbleness and wisdom, to try to deflect the spotlight to his players, sometimes only a day or two after he had gone out of his way to deflect that same spotlight and its accompanying pressure in a different direction to protect them.

"I worry sometimes that people might perceive him as cold and uncaring," says one long-time athletic administrator who worked with him for just a few years. "He's a very private man who is so dedicated to what he is doing that he can shut off

Above: Holtz always had a reputation for getting the most from his talent, partly through his ability as an organizer, but largely through his intense motivational techniques which often included tears.

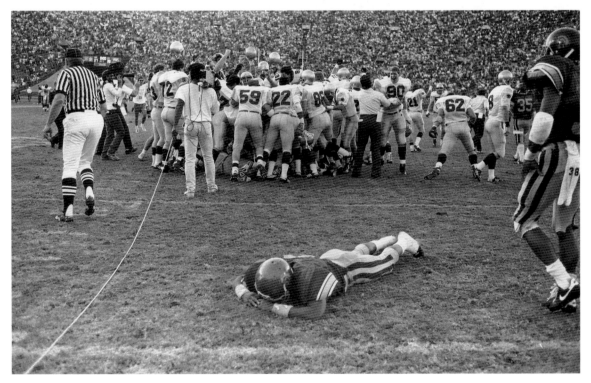

Left: Holtz endeared himself to Irish fans in his first season as his team defeated arch-rival USC in the final seconds, 38-37, at the Los Angeles Coliseum. An unidentified Trojan player sobs on the ground after the winning ND field goal.

Right: *Holtz counted among his motivational tricks the art of magic, and says he believes games sometimes are won "by miracles, but not by the coaches."*

the outside world. He just refuses to be unprepared about anything, whether it's a game or a speech. He hates free-lancing. He just really punishes himself."

But Holtz has always punished himself in his coaching career because he has the same intensity and commitment to the game that motivates all great football coaches. His talent for thorough organization, his instinctive teaching skills, his ability to judge and use personnel correctly and an insecurity that forces him to work long hours and still feel he could do more have driven him to succeed, in some form or other (he's had five losing seasons in his career, including his first one at Notre Dame) at every school that has hired him.

Holtz always started every program with an insistence on team play. When he came to Notre Dame, he handed out T-shirts with "Team" in big letters and "me" in small type. When he met the Irish players for the first time as a team, he tossed out one of his famous Holtz-isms: "Do what is right, do the best you can and treat others like you want to be treated," and then he fired the important salvo: "First we will be best, then we will be first." He lives by these *bon mots:* "You either get

Right: *Tony Rice quarterbacked Holtz's 1988 national championship team at Notre Dame and just missed another national championship in 1989 when the Irish lost their final game of the regular season to eventual champion Miami.*

better or worse. You never stay the same . . . If what you did yesterday seems big, you haven't done anything today."

Holtz does something big every day. He is a hands-on coach, making tart corrections in practice sessions if players make what he considers "easy mistakes." He'll step into a group of towering offensive linemen and, with a cutting, slashing flood of words that can crush anyone's ego, correct an improper blocking technique. His assistant coaches could do the correcting, but Holtz obviously feels the matter is only dealt with to his satisfaction if he does it himself.

Part of his philosophy is that if you put enough pressure on players during practice, and drive them hard enough and make them intense enough during the week, then game days will be a treat. He drills and fusses and repeats and drives them, and

does it in every workout. One of his players once quipped, "We'll get this two-hour practice right, even if it takes six hours."

"I am a teacher," Holtz has said. "I love to be an active coach, and instruct the players. But I wish I was more patient. If I was murdered as soon as practice is over, there would be so many suspects among the players that they wouldn't even try to investigate."

All of this has paid off, as he has averaged more than eight victories a year, and with the exception of Arkansas where he succeeded Broyles and, in a sense, at Notre Dame, where his predecessor Gerry Faust had a winning record but really was at the end of his tether at South Bend (he lost his final game 58-7 to the University of Miami) his hallmark has been in bringing losing schools back to football life, and making them winners.

Above: *Holtz's 1988 team defeated West Virginia in the Fiesta Bowl to win the national championship. Here, fullback Anthony Johnson pounds the Mountaineers' defense early in that game.*

HOWARD JONES

Record:

Syracuse (1908)	6-3-1
Yale (1909)	10-0-0
Ohio State (1910)	6-1-3
Yale (1913)	5-2-3
Iowa (1916-23)	42-17-1
Duke (1924)	4-5-0
So. California (1925-40)	121-36-13

Howard Jones never used an epithet stronger than "goldang," "ye gads" or "pshaw." He forbade his players to take advantage of a rival player's injury. Yet he carried on a career-long feud with two of the lions of college football: Knute Rockne and Pop Warner.

A former player observed: "Howard Jones was a persistent, aggressive driver of himself and his players who lived football, but who lacked imagination and creative ability, yet had the ability to recognize real ability in his players." Other observers have noted that Howard Jones' mind was tracked so firmly into football that he ignored traffic signals and other cars as he drove, lost socks and keys, forgot appointments, left members of his family stranded, and sometimes even forgot his way home.

This is a strange but accurate picture of perhaps college football's most unsung Hall of Fame coach, who spanned the game from its Americanization at the turn of the century at Yale, through its era of great coaches and innovators, to the door of its modernization prior to World War II – and in the process won 194 games.

It is difficult to understand how a man who was so sensitive, demanding, perceptive, talented, and successful does not occupy a pedestal alongside his contemporaries Rockne, Warner, Stagg, Zuppke, Yost, Bierman, Wade and Sutherland, whose memories are hallowed but all of whom he defeated with some regularity. His five Rose Bowl victories still are a record. He also has to his credit three national championships, as well as ten major conference championships.

In 1909, as Yale's first paid coach (he had been a star end there at the turn of the century), Jones' team was unbeaten and unscored-upon in ten games. Some of Yale's greatest players – Ted Coy, John Reed Kilpatrick and Steve Philibin – were on that team, and they even beat his former Syracuse team, coached by his brother, Tad, who would later become one of Yale's greatest coaches. When Jones returned for a second tour of duty, in 1913, he was voted a $2500 annual salary.

Above: *Howard Jones won a record five Rose Bowl games at Southern California during his 16 seasons as head coach, and is second on the school's all-time victory list with 116.*

Right: *Jones' first head coaching job was at Yale, where his 1909 team was unbeaten and unscored-upon. He was the school's first paid head coach.*

Left: *Duke Slater is considered one of Iowa's greatest linemen. A guard on the 1921 team, he helped end Notre Dame's 22-game winning streak, a career highlight for Jones.*

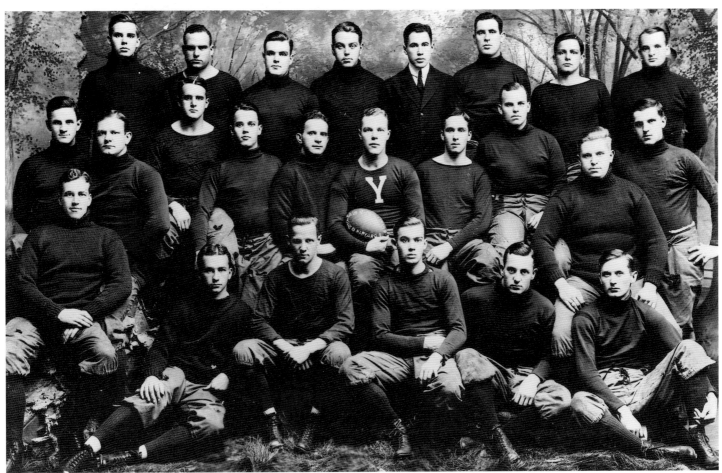

Jones made his first big coaching impact when he went to Iowa in 1916, and five years later, coached the first of two consecutive Big Ten champions, the only unbeaten teams in the school's history. His 1921 team, a totally Iowa-born-and-bred unit that featured backs Glenn and Aubrey Devine, Gordon Locke and Craven Shuttleworth, and guard Duke Slater, one of the few black collegiate stars in that time, ended Notre Dame's 22-game unbeaten streak with a 10-7 victory that Jones always considered the highlight of his career.

Throughout his career, Jones was completely consumed with football. His game evolved from almost total reliance on the single wing tailback running inside the tackles – when his great teams of the late 1920s played Notre Dame, the players often told the Irish where the next play was going, and still they gained yardage – to one of the most complex in the history of the game in later years at Southern California, where good weather was conducive to more passing, sure footing and pleasant practices. He never ceased agonizing over problems until he came up with solutions, which inevitably were correct, and this made him a very tough

Right: *Gordon Locke was a member of the 1921 Iowa backfield that also included brothers Glenn and Aubrey Devine, and Craven Shuttleworth. The Hawkeyes were unbeaten in seven games that season as part of a school-record 21-game winning streak.*

Left: *Jones lectures his 1932 Southern Cal team that won all 10 of its games, including a 35-0 victory over Pitt in the Rose Bowl.*

Below: *Cotton Warburton, later an Oscar-winning cinematographer, was the star of Jones' 1938 and 1939 teams that won back-to-back Rose Bowls against Duke and Tennessee, respectively, neither of which had given up a point until those games.*

and canny coach to contend with.

A good example of his knack for problem-solving came during the 1932 Rose Bowl, when his Southern Cal Trojans played Bernie Bierman's Tulane Green Wave. He knew that Jerry Dalrymple, Tulane's right end, often abandoned his defensive area to follow plays to the other side. Jones had a pet reverse featuring left end Ray Sparling, and he figured that Dalrymple would track him as he moved right to take a handoff and attempt a sweep. So he added another wrinkle – a double reverse, in which Sparkling took the ball, but then handed it to Ernie Pinckert going back toward the left. The original reverse scored a touchdown, though Dalrymple had followed Sparling. At the half, Jones ordered the new double reverse, and, with Dalrymple blocked out as he moved with Sparling, Pinckert scored twice on runs of 30 and 27 yards in a 21-12 victory.

In 1931, Southern Cal played at Notre Dame in the final game of the season and the Irish were on a 25-game unbeaten streak. Gaius Shaver's two fourth-quarter touchdowns had trimmed a 14-0 Notre Dame lead to 14-13 with four minutes to play, when Jones' coaching genius struck again. Shaver completed a 50-yard pass to Sparling, the first by USC in the game, and on the next play Jones ordered a shift that made left tackle Bob Hall an eligible receiver. The Irish missed the change and Hall caught a 24-yard pass to Notre Dame's 17-yard line. Three plays later, with the Irish expecting a pass, Johnny Baker kicked a 23-yard field goal to win the game.

After the game, Southern California was awarded the first Rockne Trophy as it won its second national championship under Jones. But more important to Jones that day was getting directions to the cemetery near South Bend where

Above: *Jack Banta, later an outfielder with the Brooklyn Dodgers, gains 10 yards against Duke in the 1939 Rose Bowl. USC won the game in the final minute on a pass from Doyle Nave to Al Krueger.*

Rockne was buried, and an hour later, Jones and his players held their own graveside tribute to his once-fierce rival.

This was in the midst of Jones' first great seasons at USC. They had won their first national championship in 1928, and like his great teams at Iowa, his starters usually played the entire game. Jones, who was a member of the All-America board, named his eleven 1928 starters on his ballot. In 1929, his 9-2 team averaged 41 points a game, then buried Sutherland's Pitt Panthers, 47-14, for his first Rose Bowl victory.

His third national championship came in 1932, during a 27-game unbeaten streak that stretched from 1931 to 1933. His 1932 team allowed just 13 points, shutting out seven opponents plus unbeaten Pitt, 35-0, in the Rose Bowl. His 1933 team shut out five of its first six opponents the following year, until Stanford ended the unbeaten string.

His teams won five Pacific Coast Conference titles in six years (1927-32), and this dominance became a bone of contention between himself and the far more celebrated Pop Warner, who then had great teams at Stanford. Jones lost the first two times their teams met (once when an extra point bounced off the helmet of end Red Badgro), tied the third, and then won the last five, four of them

shutouts. He literally ran Warner out of the Pacific Coast Conference, because of Stanford alumni discontent over his failure to beat the Trojans. To the usually non-vindictive Jones, this was sweet comeuppance, because Warner's Carlisle team had beaten his first team at Syracuse, then raised a public furor that he had used an unethical shift.

His second great era at Southern Cal came in the three years prior to his sudden death in 1941. His 1938 and 1939 teams had so much talent that he alternated two teams every other quarter. They won back-to-back Rose Bowls against Duke and Tennessee, neither of which had allowed a point during the season, with such stars as Doyle Nave – his touchdown pass to Al Krueger in the final minute defeated Duke 7-3 in the 1939 Rose Bowl – Cotton Warburton, later a famous movie director (John Wayne, then known as Duke Morrison, was a tackle on one of his early teams), Jack Banta (later an outfielder for the Brooklyn Dodgers), Ambrose Schindler and Granville Landsdell. His unbeaten 1940 team defeated Tennessee 14-0 in the 1940 Rose Bowl on touchdowns by Schindler and Krueger.

When Jones passed away suddenly from a heart attack in the spring of 1941, football lost much more than a great tactician.

FRANK LEAHY

Record:

Boston College (1939-40)	20-2-0
Notre Dame (1941-43)	24-3-3
(1946-53)	63-8-6

The Master.

Francis William Leahy earned that accolade because football rarely has known a man of his talents – a meticulous planner, a relentless taskmaster and an energetic innovator. Nor has it seen such dramatic results over such a relatively short career: seven undefeated teams in 15 seasons, four national champions, a 39-game unbeaten streak, and four Heisman Trophy winners. His mannerisms delighted the Notre Dame alumni and subway fans; often puzzled his associates; confounded his critics; and infuriated his detractors.

To Notre Dame fans, Leahy once was the Second Coming of Rockne, and his achievements were so similar to the man who had been his mentor that it was a bit spooky. Rockne compiled a record of 105 victories, 12 losses and three ties during 13 seasons as Notre Dame's head coach, for the game's best all-time winning percentage of .897. Leahy also coached 13 seasons (two at Bos-

ton College) and won 107 games, lost 13 and tied nine for a .892 mark, second-best in the sport's history. (His 87-11-9 record at Notre Dame produced an .887 mark).

The Rock and The Master were further intertwined. Rockne convinced Leahy to attend Notre Dame and play football rather than pursue a promising boxing career; Rockne's coaching had lit a fire in Leahy's soul; Leahy played tackle on Rockne's undefeated 1929 national championship team and though injuries cost him the 1930 season, his doggedness to stay and coach the "B" team caught Rockne's attention. Rockne saw a reflection of himself in Leahy and brought him to the Mayo Clinic where they shared a room while Leahy had a knee repaired and Rock had his health rehabilitated. For hours each day, Rockne tutored him on the fine points of coaching, finally tossing him a packet of six job openings he had received. "Take your pick," he told Leahy.

Leahy chose the line coaching job at Georgetown, and a decade later he was, like Rockne, head football coach at Notre Dame. There, later success aside, the comparisons ended. Leahy never achieved Rockne's stature as a national celebrity, whose name was a byword even beyond the world of sports. Leahy was an aloof, often withdrawn person who didn't have Rockne's magnetism, keen sense of humor or the ability to spellbind audiences. Rockne could beat opponents regularly

Below left: Frank Leahy played tackle for Rockne's 1929 national championship team at Notre Dame, but a knee injury cut his playing career short as a senior.

Below: Leahy was a rapt pupil of Rockne's while at Notre Dame, and became a part-time assistant during his senior year. Rockne's persuasion steered Leahy from a pro boxing career to coaching for the Irish.

Opposite top: *Leahy (second from right) won the Lambert Trophy in 1940. With him are the Lambert brothers and Boston mayor Maurice Tobin (second from left).*

Opposite bottom: *Knute Rockne's image dogged Leahy throughout his career at Notre Dame, and loomed over him in his office, as well. Leahy's career won-lost mark is second only to Rockne's.*

Above: *Leahy returned from two years of Navy duty during World War II and welcomed back a nucleus of veteran players who helped his 1946 team win the national championship. Bottom row (l to r): Jim Mello, Ziggy Czarobski, Bob McBride, Gerry Cowhig. Top row (l to r): Luke Higgins, Bob Livingstone, George Tobin, Bob Kelly.*

without their taking it personally; Leahy not only beat them, but his off-field graciousness infuriated them.

But Rockne never out-worked him, and each was a master psychologist – Leahy in the Gil Dobie mold who, regardless of his team's great talent, began every season saying: "The lads don't have it this year. I don't see how we can escape losing three games." He psyched his players on the pride and tradition of Notre Dame – that losing was embarrassing to the school, its traditions, and their families and friends. No matter how weak the next opponent, he cited enough little things that by Saturday his players were convinced they were up against the finest team in the country. When his Boston College team was travelling to New

Orleans by train to play Tulane, he moaned about how much work it was missing; when Idaho was coming to South Bend by train to play the Irish, he moaned about how much rest the Vandals were getting while his team was practicing.

While Rockne talked in machine-gun-like fashion, Leahy talked in square root. He referred to himself in the editorial "we," and addressed his squad as "lads." He usually called a player by his full name, and even his criticisms were delivered with a flourish. Quarterback Frank Tripucka once fumbled a snap just before the half, with the Irish ahead 14-0. "Francis, oh Francis, you hate me," Leahy intoned en route to the locker room. "You hate Notre Dame. What did I do that you do this to me, Francis? I like you Francis. Why do you hate me, Francis?"

In 1942, he shocked Irish fans by junking Rockne's famed Notre Dame shift for the T-formation, saying, "If Rockne was here, he'd be the first to try it. Besides, material, coaching, blocking and tackling – not systems – win football games."

So did toughness. He picked his linemen by taking the seven roughest, toughest men on the squad, regardless of position. Fullbacks came to Notre Dame and played tackle; halfbacks became

Above: *Leahy returned to his alma mater as head coach in 1941 and was named Coach of the Year after going unbeaten. He stunned Irish followers by junking the hallowed Notre Dame Box for the T formation.*

ends; tackles became guards. Leahy's litmus test was putting a defense on the field, telling it what play was coming, and then ordering the offense to move the ball. At one practice, one of his freshmen was cut down by a thunderous block from end Leon Hart. The first thing the dazed youngster heard was Leahy's voice from his tower: "God bless you, Leon. God bless you."

He drove himself harder than his coaches and players, often working 18-hour days. At one stretch, he was home only six days in a 90-day period; during the season, he was home just two nights a week. But his practice sessions were con-

ducted in an efficient, businesslike manner. His worst enemy was complacency, and his defense against it was driving his players to perfection. In the end, this drive consumed him to the point that while Notre Dame was in the midst of ending Georgia Tech's 31-game unbeaten streak in 1953, he collapsed at halftime.

But while he was coaching, none ever was better. His line coaching job at Georgetown so impressed Michigan State coach Jim Crowley, one of Notre Dame's famed Four Horsemen, that he hired him, and a year later took him to Fordham where Leahy developed the famed Seven Blocks of

pleading and much bad feeling, Leahy was at Notre Dame with a mandate from the Rev. John Cavanaugh, the university's vice president, to restore the Irish to the pinnacle last forged by Rockne – undefeated and Number 1. He started with an 8-0-1 season in 1941 and was named Coach of the Year; and in 1943, after losing eventual Heisman Trophy winning quarterback Angelo Bertelli to the Marines and replacing him with sophomore Johnny Lujack, another future Heisman winner, his team still came within 30 seconds of a perfect season, losing in the final game against Great Lakes after defeating four unbeaten teams.

Leahy spent two years in the Navy, and after the war, from 1946 to 1949, his teams had a 39-game unbeaten streak and three national championships, with such players as Lujack, Terry Brennan, George Connor, Bill Fisher, Marty Wendell, Ziggy Czarobski, Red Sikto and ends Jim Martin and Leon Hart, another Heismen winner. In 1946, Leahy's great crusade was to avenge a pair of 59-0 and 48-0 beatings by Army's great Blanchard and Davis teams the previous two years, but he got only a scoreless tie, which he considered a defeat. He had

Below: *Halfback Johnny Lattner, star of Leahy's 1953 unbeaten team, was one of four Heisman Trophy winners that Leahy produced. The others were Angelo Bertelli, Johnny Lujack and Leon Hart.*

Granite line that included future pro football Hall of Fame coach Vince Lombardi. Seven years later, in 1939, he succeeded Gil Dobie as head coach at Boston College. B.C. HIRES UNKNOWN LEAHY AS COACH, screamed one headline in Boston. In his first season, the "unknown" Leahy took BC to the Cotton Bowl with an 8-2 record; in his second, the Eagles were unbeaten, and defeated what many consider the best Tennessee team in history in the Sugar Bowl.

Just after Leahy signed a five-year contract to continue as BC's coach, Elmer Layden resigned at Notre Dame. Two weeks later, after some intense

Above: *Leahy's first team at Notre Dame, in 1941, took all the hurdles in its schedule, winning eight and tying one. His backfield included, from left: Steve Juzwik, Bob Hargraves, Angelo Bertelli and John Warner.*

Right: *Leahy's teams didn't lose a game for four seasons (1946-49), and won three national championships during that time. The streak was ended at 39 games by Purdue in 1950, the only season that Leahy ever lost more than two games.*

his only non-winning season in 1950 when the Irish were 4-4-1, but in his final three seasons, he lost only four games.

His 1952 team was young and inexperienced but it won seven games and tied another in ten games; and in 1953, with Heisman Trophy winner Johnny Lattner leading the way, he coached his seventh unbeaten team, winning nine games and tying one. During that 14-14 standoff against Iowa, Leahy made perhaps his biggest mistake as a coach by sanctioning a phony injury to stop the clock and help his team get its tie-making touchdown. Despite his pleas that such tactics long had been a part of the game's unwritten rules, this wasn't the way a Notre Dame team was supposed to play. More importantly, it became the final straw for some in Notre Dame's administration who had become uneasy with the team's great success, and Leahy was informed that his resignation, for health reasons, would be accepted.

In a final gesture following a very emotional farewell press conference, Leahy toured the campus, then stopped under the Golden Dome, bowed his head in prayer, and quietly blew a kiss to that ultimate Notre Dame symbol.

Knute Rockne couldn't have done it better.

DAN MCGUGIN

Record:

Vanderbilt (1904-17)	95-24-5
(1919-34)	102-31-14

Dan McGugin wasn't the first southern college football coach to use Union General William Tecumseh Sherman's famous "March to the Sea" to inspire his team against "Yankee" invaders. When the mighty Michigan Wolverines, coached by his famous brother-in-law, Fielding H. Yost, came to Nashville to help the Commodores dedicate their new stadium, in the first game of the 1922 season, he skillfully spun a pre-game tale to incite his players to a necessary superhuman effort. Pointing in the direction of a nearby cemetery, he said in a voice choking with emotion:

"Over yonder lie the heroic dead of the Confederacy, your grandfathers and your granduncles, your kin. They fought for the South, for you. They shed their blood and gave their lives to save this glorious land from the hands of the oppressors from the North. They made the last great sacrifice to come, for your generation and mine.

"Boys, this afternoon, in just a few minutes from now, you will be facing the grandsons of the men who filled those graves with our heroic Confederate dead. Their grandfathers ravaged our villages and our cities, destroyed our farms, burnt our crops, pillaged all that we possessed and made of the South a barren wasteland.

"Today, boys, the spirits of our heroic dead are looking down upon you from on high. Will you avenge them or will you let yourselves be beaten by the grandsons of the men who brought woe, misery, poverty, and death into every home of the land we hold sacred? When you face that line of dark blue out there, remember the fallen line of the heroic men in gray whose ashes now rest over yonder . . ."

And on he went, calling up every imaginable emotion. The result: Underdog Vanderbilt played a scoreless tie against one of the best Michigan teams ever coached by Yost, and spoiled a perfect season for the Wolverines. The tie also spoiled a perfect season for his own team, but that was acceptable, because it was supposed to get run out by Michigan.

All of this worked the way he planned, but he never told his players that he was raised with a different perspective on that bit of history: His grandfather, a native of Iowa like himself, had marched with Sherman. As far as his players were concerned, McGugin was Confederate born-and-bred.

To be sure, McGugin was not a master of his-

trionics or of gloom-and-doom, but one of his greatest coaching assets was the way he mixed humor, kindliness and an amazing sense of psychology to extract all that he needed from his team. On that day, he knew that his team, all lads from the South who had learned tales of the Yankee invaders from their grandparents, would make that game against Michigan a personal crusade. He had done the same thing when an under-sized Vanderbilt team played a scoreless tie against mighty Yale in 1910, and it wasn't until some time later that his players found about his Yankee heritage. They evidently forgot to tell the players who came after.

While McGugin was one of the pioneers in the growth of American football after the turn of the century, and along with Georgia Tech coach Bill Alexander helped elevate the competitive level of the game in the South, he probably was most renowned for the way he worked with his players. No

Below: Dan McGugin is the all-time winningest coach at Vanderbilt, with 197 victories in 30 seasons. He helped put southern college football on the map.

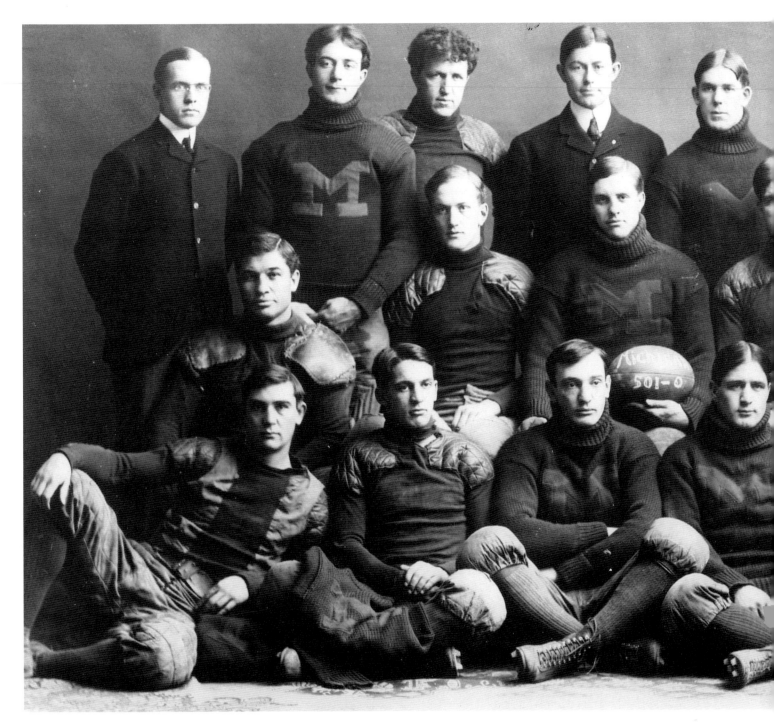

Above: *McGugin (top row, second from left) was a member of Michigan's famed 1901 "point-a-minute" team that was coached by his future brother-in-law, Fielding H. Yost.*

one ever heard him publicly bawl out a player on the practice field or during a game. He often dropped by a player's room, or called him aside elsewhere on the campus, to settle the problem. But problems didn't often crop up, his players always claimed, because they so respected McGugin that they gave a full effort every time they practiced and played.

This effort showed in McGugin's fine record. He didn't lose a game in his first season, 1904, and his team allowed just four points. His next three teams lost just one game, and none of them were scored on by a southern team. Eight other McGugin-coached teams also lost just one game in a season, while three others, in 1910 and 1921-22, were unbeaten. When the Commodores trekked to New

Haven to play Yale in 1910, McGugin used only 11 men, and the *Yale News* noted afterward: "We were lucky to hold the visitors scoreless. Vanderbilt was the fastest and best organized team seen here in years."

McGugin learned much of his coaching acumen from Yost, for whom he played guard when Michigan had its "point-a-minute" team in 1903. He had already played two years at Drake University in Iowa and graduated, then came to Michigan law school, and played two more years while earning his law degree, which he never used. Instead, he became so intrigued with football that he became an assistant to Yost for a year, then followed up a recommendation that Yost sent on his behalf to Vanderbilt. He didn't receive a reply, and a few

guards to lead the interference on sweeps. He also pioneered a speed attack in the South, as well as the forward pass; and from Yost, he brought the Michigan punting game as part of his unique "punt, pass and prayer" system that was much more organized and effective than it sounded.

The difference in style between McGugin and his old coach was dramatic, yet the two of them became close friends long before marriage brought them into the same family (Yost came to Nashville to be best man at McGugin's wedding, met the bride's sister and married her a short time later). Yost was a grim, deadly-serious person while McGugin had a warm, open personality with a keen sense of humor. But McGugin had an intense respect for his brother-in-law, as a player will have for his old coach, even if they become peers. Both men were inducted into the Hall of Fame in 1951.

When McGugin retired from coaching in 1934, the man they called "Smiling Dan," and who came from a small town in Iowa that didn't even have a high school football team, had served at one school for 30 years (counting two years of military service during World War I when one of his great stars, Ray Morrison, filled in), a record for consecutive years as a head coach at one college.

Above: *McGugin pioneered a speed attack in southern football and was the first coach to make extensive use of the forward pass. He also emphasized the punting game and the use of guards to lead sweeps.*

weeks later was invited to apply at Baldwin Wallace College in Cleveland, who accepted him and offered him $1000 per year as salary.

McGugin went to the telegraph office and wrote a message accepting the job. When he returned to his fraternity, he found a telegram from Vanderbilt offering him its job for $850 per year, so he ran back to the telegraph office, rescued his previous dispatch, and instead accepted Vanderbilt's offer. "I wanted to come to the South and see and know the people," he said later.

He became one of the South's greatest coaches, blending his keen judgment of people with a sound base of fundamentals and good teaching skills. He also was a clever strategist, one of the first to use the Statue of Liberty reverse and to allow his

JOHN MCKAY

Record:

So. California (1960-75)   127-40-8

John McKay established two great legacies at the University of Southern California during his 16 years as a head coach: His "student body right and left" offense, and the famed "USC tailback." Of course, from those came four national championships, five Rose Bowl victories in eight trips, 25 All-America players, two Heisman Trophy winners and eight conference championships.

McKay led the Trojans through a golden era during the 1960s and for half of the 1970s with one great team after another, all of them keyed by superb running backs such as Mike Garrett, O. J. Simpson, and Anthony Davis; big, mobile offensive lines; and often a splashy wide receiver such as

Below: *John McKay was an assistant coach at USC for only a year before getting the top job in 1960. He stayed for 16 seasons and became the school's all-time winningest coach.*

Lynn Swann. To the delight of Southern Cal fans, these teams went through a 14-year period when they had a 9-4-1 record against crosstown rival UCLA, and an 8-4-2 mark against Notre Dame, their two biggest adversaries.

McKay's Southern Cal team represented a sun-drenched Los Angeles Coliseum when almost everyone else was beginning to shiver from winter's cold; sun-tanned, blonde-haired co-eds who seemed destined for nearby Hollywood; Tommy Trojan riding his famed horse; and a

maroon-jerseyed team with bright gold numerals always running off tackle or around end, often with spectacular results.

Those results were the result of McKay's decision that he would recruit the very best running back he could find, line him up in the I-formation, or occasionally shift into a split backfield, have the quarterback either toss or hand him the ball, allow the offensive line to forge some openings, and then let natural talent take its course. Of course, it was not all that simple, because McKay had 32 versions

of that "student body right and left" in his USC playbook, but no matter who ran it, the results always seemed to be about the same.

"I think a coach has to have a great deal of confidence in his system and keep refining it," McKay said, "and I had confidence in the I. It was very versatile. We shifted out of it a lot; we used motion before motion was very popular. I stayed with the power-I because I knew it could work, and I knew the players could adapt to it."

They certainly did. Garrett, who won the Heis-

Above: QB Pete Beathard scores a touchdown against Wisconsin in the 1963 Rose Bowl, the first of five victories in that game by McKay's USC teams.

Below: *O.J. Simpson was the most famous of the USC tailbacks who played for McKay, and won the Heisman Trophy in 1968. Here, he gains yards against Notre Dame in a 1967 game.*

man Trophy in 1965, gained 3221 yards in three seasons; Simpson, the 1968 Heisman winner, rolled up 3423 yards in just two seasons; Clarence Davis, who followed Simpson, had 2323 in two; and Anthony Davis set a new school record with 3724 yards.

There was no formula for playing tailback in McKay's system because Sam Cunningham, who handled the job for a year before returning to fullback, and Ricky Bell, who was the starting tailback in McKay's final season of 1975, were big; Anthony Davis and Garrett were comparatively small; Clarence Davis was simply tough; and Simpson had everything – speed, power, stamina and heart.

McKay's teams also had great depth and he was an unfaltering exponent of frequent substitution. He divided his team into three units – red, gold, and green. The red unit played the first five minutes of every quarter; the gold the next four minutes; the green the next three; after which the red returned for the last three and moved directly into the next five minutes of the next quarter, meaning that an opponent saw McKay's top unit for two five-minute stretches and two eight-minute stretches during

Left: *Tailback Mike Garrett was USC's first Heisman Trophy winner, in 1965, under McKay and helped to popularize the "student body right and left" ground game.*

the game. "I often had qualms about taking out a unit that was moving successfully," he said, "but I had confidence in our system, and wouldn't stray from it. I also was deadly afraid of getting caught with tired players when our opponent had fresh ones."

This unit system paid off spectacularly in the 1963 Rose Bowl game against Wisconsin, when fresh waves of USC troops rolled to a 42-14 fourth quarter lead, giving McKay's team enough of a cushion to withstand a spectacular comeback by Badgers quarterback Ron VanderKellen before the Trojans escaped with a 42-37 victory.

That victory climaxed McKay's first undefeated national championship season, after he had scraped through with 4-6 and 4-5-1 records in his first two years. He fully expected to be fired after that second season because he had seen his old coach and first boss, Jim Aiken, get canned at Oregon by pressure from overzealous alumni who wouldn't tolerate just one losing year after two very good ones.

"There was hardly a ripple on the water at USC," McKay said. "I had every opportunity to build my team and I appreciated the confidence."

Five years later, in 1967, he won his second national championship with a 10-1 record, including a 14-3 victory over Indiana in the Rose Bowl. McKay won a classic match against UCLA, 21-20, that matched Heisman Trophy winner Gary Beban against Simpson. Simpson's 13-yard run gave USC a 14-7 halftime lead, and after UCLA went ahead 20-14 on two touchdown passes by Beban in the second half, Simpson roared 77 yards for a tie-making, fourth-quarter touchdown and Rikki Aldrich kicked the winning extra point.

In 1972, Anthony Davis sparked a late season surge toward a third national title, returning the opening kickoff against Notre Dame for a 97-yard TD, and scoring two more on short runs for a 19-10 halftime lead. He got another TD in the third quarter before Notre Dame closed to within 25-23, but Davis then took the ensuing kickoff 96 yards for his fifth touchdown, and added the sixth in the last

Opposite top: *McKay played college football at Oregon with Hall of Famer Norm Van Brocklin, and later coached there before moving to USC. His players declared that he had a profound influence on their lives on and off the field.*

Opposite bottom: *McKay's USC teams loved to run the ball, but also made efficient use of the pass for a balanced offense. Here, Anthony Davis carries for the Trojans in 1973.*

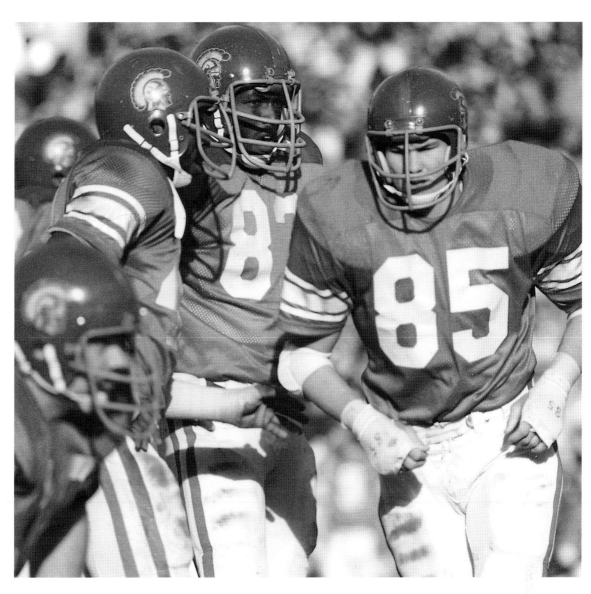

quarter as the Trojans finally won the game, 45-23. McKay's team broke a 7-7 halftime tie in the Rose Bowl as Cunningham unveiled his famous "Sam Bam" leaps into the end zone for four second-half touchdowns and Davis scored another in a 42-17 victory.

McKay's final bit of glory before he headed for the NFL and the expansion Tampa Bay Buccaneers came in 1974 with his fourth national title (by UPI) with a 10-1-1 record. It included an 18-17 victory over Ohio State in the Rose Bowl a month after the Trojans rebounded from a 24-0 halftime deficit against Notre Dame by scoring an astounding 55 points in the first 17 minutes of the second half, 26 by Anthony Davis, to come away with a 55-24 victory. They won the Rose Bowl in the final two minutes on Pat Haden's touchdown pass to J. K. McKay, the coach's son, followed by his two-point conversion pass to Sheldon Diggs.

McKay also developed a reputation as a master quipster, sometimes more acerbic than humorous, particularly when things were going awry. He also had a reputation for hard work, something that he learned back in his native Everettsville, West Vir-ginia, in Appalachia, the coal-mining region of the state, during the Depression days of the mid-1930s. His father died when he was 13 and he swept out the town's general store every morning before school, and then worked in the coal mines for a year after he graduated from high school. He spent four years in the Air Force, playing halfback on the base team, and then enrolled at Purdue at age 23. He played with the Boilermakers for a year, then transferred and finished his college eligibility at Oregon, playing with Hall of Fame quarterback Norm Van Brocklin on a team that went to the Cotton Bowl in 1948.

He coached for Aiken and Len Casanova at Oregon, then went to USC to work for Don Clark in 1959. Clark was fired at the end of the season and McKay was appointed as his successor. From that point he began to rebuild USC football to a point that Mike Garrett once described as "creating the Golden Dome effect of South Bend in Southern California out of the residue of his character. He affected the lives of hundreds of football players at USC, and that tradition will be at USC for a very long time."

Above: *McKay's big defensive squad supported his outstanding offensive units, which McKay rotated to keep the players fresh.*

JESS NEELY

Record:

SW Tennessee (1924-27)   20-17-2
Clemson (1931-39)   43-35-7
Rice (1940-66)   144-124-10

In 1965, a wire service dispatch from Houston noted: "Somebody made the remark at mathematics-minded Rice University that the school's esteem for veteran football coach Jess Neely 'rises exponentially.' School president Kenneth Pitzer said he figures if the factor is two, that would mean the esteem for Neely would be 30 million times more than when he became coach 25 years ago."

That would be about the right amount for a man who gave 40 years to coaching college football, and indeed it was just what everyone ever connected with Neely felt was a minimum tribute to a coach who had brought both Clemson and Rice to superstar status among college football powers, and had done it under rather harsh conditions – at Clemson, there was no money, and at Rice there were few blue-chip student-athletes and stringent academic requirements as well as poor facilities.

Yet, Neely was unwavering in his sense of duty and in nine seasons at Clemson, he had a 43-37-5 record, and took the Tigers to their first bowl game, where his 1939 team defeated Frank Leahy's Boston College team 6-3 in the 1940 Cotton Bowl. The next year he began a 27-year career at Rice University in Houston where he had a 144-124-10 record, as well as four Southwest Confer-

ence titles and six post-season games, including victories in his first three appearances.

This is not a bad record for someone who had graduated from law school and intended to be a lawyer after a great football career at Vanderbilt University under legendary coach Dan McGugin. But the law career got sidetracked forever when, during his first job as a law clerk, he was asked to coach the high school football team in Murfreesboro, Tennessee. Years later, Neely would tell his players, "I finished with a law degree, so don't do what I did. Don't be a coach." Then he would quickly add: "But I've had much satisfaction from coaching. I've been very fortunate."

The satisfaction that Neely derived from coaching football was compensation for all of the work and frustration he also had to endure in his dual task as athletic director at both Clemson and Rice. When he went to Clemson in 1931 after serving as an assistant coach on Wallace Wade's great Alabama teams for four years (he had also been head coach at Southwestern Tennessee College, now Rhodes, from 1924 to 1927) facilities were limited, as were funds to provide for any aid to prospective student-athletes. In fact, the athletic department had access to only one car, and Neely always noted "just one brake, the right one, worked properly." Clemson was a military school at the time and that didn't help in recruiting, either.

Neely took the job expecting to make Clemson a national power, but after three or four years of beating the bushes and having to beg players to attend, he wondered if his dream would end up as a nightmare. Things were so tight that he and his coaches, Bob Jones and Frank Howard, served as part-time groundskeepers. They set up the stands after practice on Friday, and Saturday morning

Right: Jess Neely brought Clemson to national prominence in the 1930s before moving to Rice University, where he became that school's all-time winningest coach, despite having the fewest students in the Southwest Conference.

Left: *Neely (second from left, kneeling) and his final coaching staff at Rice in 1966. Before leaving the school, he was responsible for building its 76,000-seat stadium and a gym.*

before the games; they cut the grass and lined the fields. They repaired all of the old equipment so it could be used again to cut costs and were ticket managers for every sporting event on the campus. They even ran Clemson's campus soda fountain, the Canteen.

Finally, some Clemson alumni, led by Rupert Fike, a Clemson graduate and cancer specialist in Atlanta, recognized Neely's difficulties, and helped to organize a fund-raising organization that became known as IPTAY, or I Pay Ten (Dollars) A Year. The fund garnered $1600 the first year and from

that point on, Clemson athletics, particularly football, began to improve as funding grew each year and helped to provide needed facilities.

When Neely's team won the 1940 Cotton Bowl, Rice beckoned him, and he admitted that leaving Clemson was tough because all of his hard work had just begun to pay off. When he went to Rice, he found almost identical conditions, except that he also had to live with very stringent academic requirements and the smallest enrollment of any major university in the country (1600 to 1800, including co-eds). Yet he was undaunted. "Our presi-

Below: *Neely brought Clemson its first bowl victory when his 1939 team (seen here) defeated Boston College 6-3 in the Cotton Bowl. His Rice teams also won three bowl games in a row after he became head coach in 1940.*

Above: *Dick Moegle was the centerpiece in Rice's 28-6 victory over Alabama in the 1954 Cotton Bowl. He gained 265 yards rushing on 11 carries and scored three TDs, one after 'Bama's Tommy Lewis jumped off the bench and tackled him as he broke into the clear.*

Above right: *Neely retired as Rice's football coach and athletic director in 1967, and then spent 10 years as athletic director at Vanderbilt.*

dent told me, 'Don't bring anybody in who isn't in the upper half of his class, and has at least eight quality credits,'" Neely recalled. "That eliminated a lot of athletes.

"Most of the boys we brought in were interested in an education, and enjoyed playing football. But they were at Rice primarily to get an education and playing football was strictly secondary. My recruiting pitch was the same with each boy. I felt our school was offering him a marvelous opportunity and in return I expected him to rearrange his priorities so that his first responsibility was to get his degree. Secondly, I expected him to conduct himself under our rules and to try as best he could to contribute his talents toward helping us win football games. Believe it or not, we usually got along famously. Something must have worked because we won our share of games."

He had some special ones too, and he always was proud to note that all but one player – who couldn't pass the eye test – from his 1942 team enlisted in the Marine Corps during World War II. His football program continued because Rice was part of the Navy V-12 training program, and in 1943, his Owls lost to Texas 58-0. The following year, with primarily the same players on each team, Neely played at Texas and Rice won 7-0. When he returned to play the Longhorns the next year, he dissuaded his wife from making the trip, telling her, "I think we slipped up on them last year and it may get nasty this time." Things did get nasty – for Texas, because Rice again won 7-0. In 1946, Texas visited Rice, with their great star Bobby Layne, and Neely had many of his 1942 players back. He won for a third straight year, 18-13. Three years later, Rice went to Austin and beat the Longhorns 17-15 when All-America end Froggy Williams kicked the winning field goal.

The most memorable game his Rice team ever played probably was the 1954 Cotton Bowl against Alabama when Tommy Lewis, Alabama's captain, jumped from the bench, ran onto the field and tackled Dick Moegle as he was running for a touchdown. The incident has long been remembered as one of football's great "oddities."

"The first thing you do when you have a boy break a big play is to look for any flags," Neely recalled. "He seemed to be going for a good gain, so I decided to check for the flags. When I looked back downfield a second time, Dickie suddenly went down. I thought, 'My goodness, what has happened to that boy now?' Then I saw the fellow who tackled him slip off the field. I was quite surprised. Moegle was tackled about midfield, and the referee, Cliff Shaw, walked over, picked up the ball, didn't say a word, and placed it on the two-yard line for the extra point. He ruled it an automatic 96-yard touchdown."

All of this eventually paid off at Rice as it had at Clemson because under Neely's direction as athletic director, the school built Rice Stadium (capacity 76,000) and Rice Gym in 1950, and continued its post-season success with five more bowl appearances before Neely finally resigned in 1966 and returned to his alma mater, Vanderbilt, where he was athletic director for five years. And just to keep himself occupied with the athletes, he also coached the golf team until he retired in 1981 – after 56 academic years.

"The most pleasure you get out of coaching is working with youngsters, seeing them develop, then seeing them graduate, and following the success that most of them have throughout their lives," Neely said.

That meant as much to him as his induction into the National Football Foundation's Hall of Fame.

GEN. ROBERT R. NEYLAND

Record:

Tennessee (1926-34) 76-7-5

(1936-40) 43-7-3

(1946-52) 54-17-4

The Corps of Cadets at West Point was happily engaged at dinner in the giant mess hall on the evening of September 13, 1913, when orders were suddenly read out that Cadet Corporal Robert R. Neyland and eight others "are confined to the barracks, the area of the barracks and the gymnasium until April 10, 1914 and will serve punishment tours at the usual required hours. . . . "

Neyland had been "slugged" for what authorities considered unauthorized hazing of a plebe, and though he had been hazed the same way the previous year without any punishment meted out, Neyland accepted the consequences and decided to make the best of it. He took up boxing for the first time, to the jeers of some classmates, and declared, "I'll win the heavyweight championship before I leave here."

Before the year ended, he did win it; and before he graduated from West Point he also tacked on a pair of varsity football letters, playing with such future military heroes as Dwight D. Eisenhower, Omar Bradley and James Van Fleet, and established a record 22-game winning streak as the baseball team's best pitcher while posting a 36-5 career record, which earned him a $3500 pro offer.

That was just a preview of things to come, because Robert Reese Neyland always would be as successful in athletics as he was determined to succeed in his military career, and he built the latter around three different tours, totalling 21 years, as head coach at Tennessee. Before he sought and received an appointment to head the ROTC department at Tennessee, he served a duty tour at West Point as aide to Superintendent Douglas A. MacArthur and helped to coach the football team. In his first nine-year tour of duty at Tennessee, he was in charge of the ROTC, Chief of Army Engineers in the Tennessee River Department and head football coach.

The Army sent him to the Panama Canal Zone in 1935, and he never expected to return to coaching. But family illness and a longing to coach football again induced him to retire from the Army a year later, and he returned to Tennessee where he coached full-time until he was recalled to the service in 1941 as World War II loomed. He served until the spring of 1946, and during the war, he commanded Advance Section I in Kunming, China

as a brigadier general before finally retiring and returning to Tennessee for a third time. He won a national championship in 1951, the year before failing health forced his retirement.

Neyland also had a degree in engineering from MIT, and he applied the slide-rule techniques of his military profession to the strategies of his football teams, to which he added the rigorous discipline that he instilled in his troops to build teams which were relentless in their blocking and tackling. He was no "by the book only" coach, though, because his innovations helped to revolutionize football in the South. He was the first to do many things now taken for granted, such as using phones from the press box to the bench, developing a protective pocket for his passer, using a six-man defensive line, tear-away jerseys, and the fake pass and run.

His playbook was the leanest of any coach in the country, no more than two dozen plays in any year, but each of them was drawn and run with an engineer's precision. He rarely used more than 16 plays in a game, a throwback to his days at West Point when his coach, Charley Daly, preached

Below: *Robert R. Neyland was a star at West Point before entering the Army. He also was an assistant coach for Army before going to Tennessee in 1926 as head of the school's ROTC department and its football coach.*

Right: *Bobby Dodd (right) was the best quarterback ever to play for Neyland and later became a great head coach and competitor for rival Georgia Tech.*

Right: *Bowden Wyatt, an All-America end, was the greatest defensive player ever to play for Neyland, who stressed defense over offense. Wyatt later was a head coach at Tennessee.*

quality over quantity. "The average quarterback can't think of more than 20 during a game," Neyland said. "When his mind is overloaded, it hurts the entire team.

"But no play really is any good until it is rehearsed at least 500 times," he added. "A poorly designed play, well-executed, is much better than a well-designed play, poorly executed."

He proved that theory while an assistant coach at West Point when he devised a forward pass to be thrown off a reverse that the unbeaten Cadets would use against Navy. He was not satisfied until it had been rehearsed more than 100 times, but it worked the three times it was used in the Army-Navy game, and set up scores each time.

At Tennessee, 90 percent of his offense consisted of off-tackle plays, line bucks, two reverses, a fake run and pass, a fake pass and run, a quarterback sneak, and a half-dozen passes, all run from the single wing formation to which he adhered through his final game in 1952. Observers said that Neyland could send his playbook to an opposing coach and still be successful because of his team's flawless execution of the plays. Before the Orange Bowl game against Oklahoma in 1938, a newspaper published a complete diagram of his pet reverse play, detailing every assignment, and Neyland worried that the Sooners would stop it. He called the play for the first time ten minutes into the game and Bob Foxx ran eight yards, untouched, for a touchdown.

What made the Vols so volatile was a fearsome reliance on blocking, which was awesome in its execution. In a game against Mississippi, Buist Warren returned a punt 85 yards for a touchdown, and films showed than ten Ole Miss players lay flat on the ground and one other staggered to his feet at the end of the play.

"A lot of boys know how to block, but few know when to block," Neyland said. "It's all in the timing. Our boys block, block, block every afternoon, and they either get good at it or they give up football. The best ball carrier in the country couldn't play for us if he couldn't block."

While his offense always was crisp and efficient, he was most renowned for his defense which allowed less than a touchdown a game during his entire career. Again, his playbook was sparse – a basic 6-2-2-1 alignment was all his Volunteers needed for most of his coaching career. But the results proved that what a team uses isn't as important as how it uses what it has, which underscored his belief that it was easier to score on defense than on offense. "Even if your attack is stopped, you still have five ways to score – intercepted pass, safety, blocked kick, punt return and fumble recovery – if you are trained for it, and are defense-minded," he said.

His teams were tenacious in this regard, taking their cue from his oft-repeated motto: "It has been said there is guts at both ends of a bayonet, but there is guts, too, at both ends of a tackle."

His defense went through the equivalent of "live" bayonet practice every day of the season, and it paid off, because his team shut out its opponents in more than half of the 216 games he coached. His 1939 team didn't allow a point in 10 regular season games. The Vols put an end to Southern Cal's 15-game scoreless streak in the Rose Bowl that year. In 1938, 1939, and 1940, only five teams scored against Tennessee.

This was one of two great eras of football during Neyland's reign at Knoxville, when his team became the first ever to be invited to three different post-season games in as many years as they ran off a streak of 31 consecutive regular season games without a loss, with great players like Bowden Wyatt, George Cafego and Bob Suffridge. The year after he became head coach, in 1926, his teams started a 32-game unbeaten streak, more than underlining the only mandate he received when appointed head coach: "Beat Vanderbilt!" Tennessee's cross-state rival, under Dan McGugin, had won 16 games, including six in a row. Neyland's team lost in his first season, but only twice thereafter.

If Neyland had a fault, it was his total opposition to two-platoon football in the late 1940s, and his teams continued to try and compete with one-way players until he saw his defensive excellence being eroded, and reluctantly joined the parade. But once he came across, the Vols of 1950 won 10 of 11 games and defeated Texas in the Cotton Bowl. The following year, led by All-America tailback Hank Lauricella, he won his only national championship with a 10-0 record, with the same stingy defense and the single wing offense that many were calling outmoded.

But in the very precise and demanding mind of Gen. Robert R. Neyland, precision, execution, and excellence never were outmoded.

Left: *Hank Lauricella (27) was an All-America running back for Neyland on his 1951 national championship team that won all 10 of its games with a single wing attack that many had called outmoded.*

TOM OSBORNE

Record:

Nebraska (1973-89) 168-38-2*

*Still active

Tom Osborne – "Dr. Tom" to the legions of Nebraska football fans – began the 1990 college football season with the best winning percentage among all active coaches, placing him in some heady company with Joe Paterno of Penn State, LaVell Edwards of Brigham Young, Bobby Bowden of Florida State, Dan James of Washington and Lou Holtz of Notre Dame, all of whom had been head coaches for a longer period of time.

Osborne has achieved a win-loss percentage of .832 since inheriting the job from Hall of Fame coach Bob Devaney who, as athletic director at Nebraska, is Osborne's boss. That in itself flies in the face of a bit of realism that decrees: Never be the man to follow the legendary coach; instead, follow the man who followed the legend, because no matter what the legend's successor might do, it can

Left: *Nebraska coach Tom Osborne has won over 80 percent of his games and is the top winner in Big Eight history.*

Opposite: *Bob Devaney preceded Osborne as head coach at Nebraska and won a pair of national titles. Osborne served as assistant coach under Devaney.*

Above: *Johnny Rodgers received the Heisman Trophy in 1972 after leading the Cornhuskers, under head coach Bob Devaney and assistant coach Tom Osborne, to nine victories in 11 games. He was Nebraska's first Heisman winner.*

never be better. However, the next guy coming along won't be burdened with such high expectations, and his success will be more reasonably accepted.

Osborne has run right past that dictum, and he is headed for a Hall of Fame spot right beside Devaney once he finishes coaching. He already has won more games than any coach in Big Eight Conference history, and that includes Devaney, as well as Bud Wilkinson and Barry Switzer of Oklahoma. In addition, he has won or shared seven Big Eight titles and has coached ten teams to at least ten victories in a season. All of his teams have been ranked in the top ten at season's end, and each of them has gone to post-season bowl games.

Incredibly, Osborne also is the only coach in Nebraska history ever to defeat a top-ranked team, when the Huskers defeated Oklahoma 17-14 in 1978. But he also has felt the sting of seeing his own Number 1 ranking knocked off, depriving him of a long-sought national championship. Devaney won back-to-back national titles in 1970 and 1971, and he was ready at the time to step away and turn the coaching reins over to Osborne when someone

pointed out that no coach in the game's history ever won three straight national titles. So Devaney stayed for one more season, but his dream ended in a 17-14 loss to Oklahoma in the season's final game.

Osborne got the job after that, and Devaney calls it "the best hire I ever made." He had known the young Nebraskan ever since Osborne applied for a job as a graduate assistant when a three-year playing career in the NFL with the Washington Redskins and San Francisco 49ers ended after the 1961 season.

"He simply wrangled the grad assistant job out of me," Devaney said. "I don't think we paid him a salary, just allowed him to take his meals at our team's training table, and got him a room free of charge in the dorm so he could go to school."

Osborne was working on his master's degree and then stayed on to complete his doctorate in educational psychology (in 1965). Instead of buying a couch and hanging out a shingle, he became the team's receivers coach. Over the next five years, he was in charge of the Huskers' passing game, and in his last four seasons as an assistant coach, he developed All-America back Johnny Rodgers, who became Nebraska's first Heisman Trophy winner in 1972.

When Devaney announced before the 1972 season that it would be his last, he appointed Osborne as assistant head coach and director of recruiting, hand-picking him as a successor.

Throughout most of his tenure at Nebraska, Osborne's foremost rival for a conference and national title has been Oklahoma, and while the Sooners have won both, the lack of a national title stings Osborne a bit, though never to the point of becoming a monster that must be destroyed. The closest he came was a memorable Orange Bowl game in 1984 when his top-ranked Huskers lost to the University of Miami 31-30. Nebraska once had trailed 17-0 in the game, but had fought back to within one point of a tie in the final seconds as the Huskers roared 74 yards in the final minute to punch over a touchdown and trail 31-30. Osborne could have kicked the extra point and gained a tie, probably keeping his team's Number 1 ranking and the long-coveted national championship, but he gained even more glory when he opted to try to win the game. But a pass for the two-point conversion from Turner Gill to Irving Fryar was batted away by Miami defensive back Ken Calhoun, and Nebraska lost the game and the national title.

"I never second-guessed the decision to go for the two points because there really wasn't any decision to make," he said. "That team wanted to

Left: *Quarterback Turner Gill scores the winning touchdown for Nebraska in the 1983 Orange Bowl against LSU. The Huskers won 21-20, but the following year they lost by a point when a two-point try missed in the final minute.*

Below: *Osborne gets a victory ride atop his players' shoulders after his 1983 Orange Bowl win. He has taken his teams to post-season games every season during his tenure at Nebraska, and has won eight times.*

Left: *Mike Rozier (30), 1983 Heisman Trophy winner, was the main cog in a Nebraska offense that produced more than 6500 yards and 84 touchdowns. He scored 29 TDs and averaged nearly eight yards per carry.*

Left: *Osborne's teams came at opponents on defense with as much vigor as they did on offense. He featured speed over bulk and helped the Huskers to top defensive rankings every season.*

Left: *Osborne featured a running game at Nebraska, but he integrated the pass offense to give his teams a good balance, particularly with running quarterbacks.*

prove it was one of the best ever. That was what they wanted. You can't prove that playing for a tie. I owed it to them to go for the win."

That Nebraska team was the best since Devaney's second national championship team that featured Rodgers. Osborne also had a Heisman Trophy winner on this team, running back Mike Rozier, and he keyed an offense that produced 6560 yards and 84 touchdowns, both single-season records. The team averaged 52 points a game, and Rozier scored 29 TDs and 174 points, gaining a record average of 7.81 yards per carry. During that season, Osborne got his 100th career victory against UCLA.

That great season, and a continual string of successes since that time, means that Osborne has come a long way from his boyhood dream of playing quarterback for Hastings College in Nebraska and following his father and grandfather as graduates of the school. He had been the state prep athlete of the year in 1954 and passed up major college scholarship offers to continue the family tradition at Hastings, also fulfilling his quarterback dream. In 1959, he was named state college athlete of the year, the first athlete in Nebraska history ever to win both the high school and college award. There isn't much left for him to achieve in athletics, unless it be the long-sought national collegiate football championship. Though he places more emphasis on winning each week, and taking the conference championship, there always is room for one more piece of hardware in the school's trophy case.

"I still want to see Nebraska win a national championship," he says. "Every coach wants that, but the thing doesn't dominate my life. If we never win one, it's not like I'm going to think of myself as a failure."

Hardly.

BENNIE OWEN

Record:

Washburn (1900)	6-2-0
Bethany (Kansas) (1901-04)	27-4-3
Oklahoma (1905-26)	122-54-16

Oklahoma wasn't even a state, and more resembled the Rodgers & Hammerstein's Broadway musical version, when Bennie Owen came to Norman as football coach in 1905. When he had finished his 22-year tenure in 1926, the Sooners were well-established and Owen was assured of being one of the first group of college football pioneers to be inducted into the Hall of Fame.

Owen is known as the "Father of Oklahoma Football," and that huge stadium on the Oklahoma campus, where Sooners teams of the past four decades have known so much national acclaim, is named after him. It is located on a spot that once held a fishing pond where Owen spent much of his leisure time.

Below: *Bennie Owen, the "Father of Oklahoma Football," started the gridiron program at the school even before Oklahoma became one of the contiguous 48 states.*

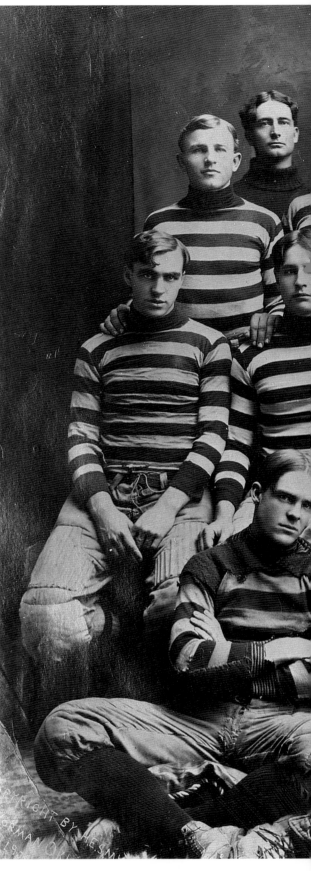

Ironically, those great Oklahoma teams which used that stadium were well-known for offenses which relied almost solely on the running game, while Owen became one of the pioneers of the forward pass in an era when some of the game's leaders claimed that for every touchdown scored

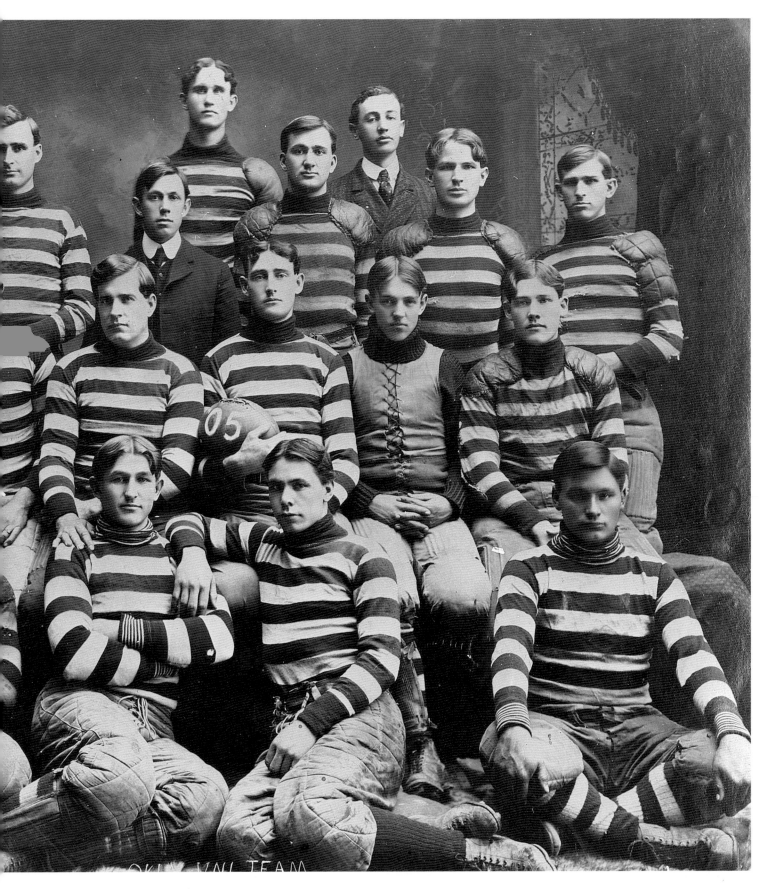

by passing, two interceptions were returned for touchdowns by the opposition.

Even more incredibly, Owen lost his right arm in a hunting accident during his third season at Norman, in 1907, the year that Oklahoma achieved statehood. This never bothered him a bit, as he went on to make the Sooners the pre-eminent team in the Southwest during the first quarter of the century.

Owen was no fly-by-night coach, having been a quarterback at Kansas under Fielding Yost for a season, and then worked for him at Michigan

Above: *Early teams like Owen's 1905 Sooners had very unique uniforms which didn't always include helmets.*

Above: *Forest (Spot) Geyer, the star of Owen's 1913 team, is still regarded as Oklahoma's greatest passer. His 25 TD passes that season remain a school record.*

first three seasons. In addition to the lack of financial resources, there also was very little high school football in the Oklahoma territory from which to draw players.

From his time at Michigan under Yost, Owen was a self-admitted "speed freak," not unlike his successors in the post-World War II era, and he always sought ways to get his fast backs into open areas. His first move was to use the direct snap from center on nearly every play, enabling his tailbacks to get a running start. Then he began to concentrate on the forward pass, which had more credibility in the Midwest, where he cut his football teeth, than in the East, where power-wedge football still was the vogue.

Many have called his Oklahoma teams of 1914-15 the Southwest's first "aerial circus," a phrase that became popular in the mid-1930s with Dutch Meyer's teams at Texas Christian University, when Sammy Baugh and Davey O'Brien hurled blizzards of footballs in every game. Meyer had played for Owen in those two seasons, when the Sooners threw the ball 30 to 35 times a game.

Owen had lost all of his regulars after the 1913 season, and decided to pin his hopes on a passing attack. Some labeled this a "wide-open, reckless game," but that season, the Sooners outscored every team in the nation. Many consider this Owen's finest coaching job – using so many untried people and still getting a 9-1-1 record. The ball at that time was shaped more like a squash than today's sleek weapon. But Forest Geyer, a gangling, blond-haired halfback who was renowned for being nonchalant on the field, became what most Oklahoma football historians believe still is the school's greatest passer – he threw 25 TD passes that season, still a school record.

The following year, 1915, Owen's team didn't lose a game – one of four undefeated teams he coached at Oklahoma – and was in the middle of a 19-game winning streak. Its great passing game masked other weaknesses, but gave it enough power to come from behind five times for victories. Defenses often assigned two defenders to end Homer Montgomery, but still Geyer found him time and time again.

Owen also was renowned for his team's clean play, in an era where fists flew freely, particularly in an emerging area of the nation where college football was in its rudimentary stages and often seemed to mirror the "law of the frontier."

Owen retired from coaching after the 1926 season to become a full-time athletic director, and later directed the intramural program until he retired in 1938. He never left Norman and died at the age of 94 in 1970 – long after Bud Wilkinson had brought more glory days to a program that began even before Oklahoma was represented by a star in the American flag.

before beginning his own coaching career, first at Washburn, and then at Bethany College in a section of Kansas where a Swedish colony had grown after the Civil War. The school quickly became famous all over the prairie for its emphasis on the arts, and particularly for its concerts featuring Handel's *Messiah*. Owen went there to discuss the coaching job with President Carl Swensson, fell in love with the school, the town and the people, and soon made the "Terrible Swedes" a football power.

His first team in 1902 was perhaps the strongest, defeating what is now Kansas State 40-0. His 1904 team was unbeaten, and drummed Oklahoma 36-9. Sooners athletic authorities were so impressed that they hired Owen, but only after he had considered a more lucrative offer from Pittsburg (Kansas) College. Owen was imbued with the pioneer spirit of the frontier, and took the challenge despite the fact that Oklahoma's program was so destitute that it still owed money to two former coaches, and he accepted IOUs on his football salary during his

ARA PARSEGHIAN

Record:

Miami (Ohio) (1951-55)	39-6-1
Northwestern (1956-63)	36-35-1
Notre Dame (1964-75)	95-17-4

The Era of Ara rivals the Age of Rockne and the Legacy of Leahy among Notre Dame's great football traditions. And the Cradle of Coaches at Miami University in Oxford, Ohio takes pride that another in its long line of famous graduates brings honor to this picturesque school set in the gently rolling hills of southwest Ohio.

Ara Raoul Parseghian learned his lessons well in that bucolic setting just as Paul Brown, Weeb Ewbank, Earl Blaik, Paul Dietzel had all done before him. But what the "Cradle" never prepared any of those men for was the terrible pressures which are the cost of the football coaching profession, and there never has been a course that pre-

pares any man to coach at Notre Dame, not even Parseghian, a man seemingly born to teach young athletes.

Parseghian, a native of Akron, Ohio, was always an intense, no-nonsense competitor, whether he was playing football at Miami, the Great Lakes Naval Training Center or for the Cleveland Browns. He got his first taste of dynamic football coaching when he played at Great Lakes in 1945 under Paul Brown, and ironically, in the final game of the 1945 season, his team upset Notre Dame, which was coached by Hugh Devore. Nearly 20 years later, he replaced Devore as the 23rd head coach at Notre Dame.

In between, Parseghian led Miami University to an unbeaten season in 1947, then played for the Cleveland Browns and Paul Brown. Injuries shortened his career, but the years he spent under Brown steered him toward the coaching profession and helped to establish many of his basic coaching principles.

Parseghian became freshman coach at Miami under Woody Hayes in 1950, and the following year, at age 27, he became the first graduate from

Below: *Ara Parseghian was a fiery, intense coach who shook up the lethargic Irish football team and brought the school a 9-1 season in his first year there as head coach (1964). He was another in a long line of great coaches to come from Miami University in Ohio.*

Previous pages: *A scene from the 1965 meeting of Notre Dame and Michigan State. The following year the game would end in a tie, spoiling Parseghian's perfect record that season.*

Above: *One of Parseghian's most dramatic victories was a 24-23 victory over Alabama in the 1973 Sugar Bowl. Here, Wayne Bullock scores the first touchdown for the Irish.*

the "Cradle" ever to return as head coach after Hayes was hired by Ohio State. From the very first day, Parseghian became a hands-on coach, very demanding and intolerant of anything or anyone who didn't share his enthusiasm or desire to excel. This attitude helped him to establish Miami's reputation as a "giant-killer" because in 1954, when his team was unbeaten, it knocked off Indiana of the Big Ten and opened the next season by defeating another Big Ten team, Northwestern, 25-14. No Miami team ever had beaten any team from the Big Ten.

Stu Holcomb, athletic director at Northwestern and a former Miami coach, felt that since he couldn't beat a team coached by Parseghian, he might as well hire him. The Wildcats had won only seven games in the four previous seasons, and were winless in 1955. But Parseghian walked blindly into a situation that was tailor-made for failure.

"I was so naive that I didn't realize Northwestern was a privately endowed school in a state conference," he said. "We didn't have the resources to compete with other Big Ten schools. My career could have ended right there."

But it didn't – because Parseghian made a bold move to conquer all of the ills which plagued Northwestern's program. His first team had a 4-4-1 record, but he knew it was hollow. So he cleaned house, cutting players with bad attitudes, and took

total command of all football matters. "It was starting from scratch," he said. "But I wasn't going to put up with people who didn't care, because there are certain sacrifices everyone must make to win. It was quite an upheaval."

He went winless in 1957, but in 1958, his efforts began to pay off. Northwestern won its first four games, including a rousing 55-24 victory over Michigan and a 21-0 victory over Ohio State. Parseghian had only one losing season during his eight years as coach, but most importantly, he defeated Notre Dame four straight games.

The Irish had five straight losing seasons when they hired Parseghian in 1964, the first non-graduate coach. He was told only one thing by the school's administration: "We don't care if you go 5-5 every season as long as you run an honest program. But if you go 10-0 and cheat, you're gone."

Parseghian didn't waste any time making his mark, going 9-1 in his first season – missing a perfect season in a 20-17 loss to Southern California in the last game of the season – with primarily the same team that had a 2-7 record the previous year. The big difference was the emergence of a third string quarterback, John Huarte, into a Heisman Trophy winner. Parseghian used the old Rockne salesmanship approach and got Huarte to believe he really was better than his ability, and then brought order to a team where the quarterback could rise above himself for that one season.

Parseghian's style incorporated Rockne's motivational quality and organizational ability, according to Ed (Moose) Krause, the athletic director at Notre Dame at the time who had played under Rockne and coached for Leahy. "Ara was a great disciplinarian, but like Rockne, his players felt they could always talk to him, not only about football but about off-field problems. They felt very close to him. Ara had the same humility that Rockne did."

Two years later, he won the national championship with a 9-0-1 record, but that one tie was a thorn that pricked him for the rest of his time at Notre Dame. The Irish and Michigan State, ranked 1-2, played in East Lansing, and the game ended in a 10-10 tie. But Parseghian was forever criticized by many Notre Dame diehards because he ended the game running out the clock and without his starting quarterback when they believed he should have been hurling passes to try and win – trying for the "magic" that always seemed to work for Rockne and Leahy.

Three years later, Notre Dame went to its first bowl game since Rockne's 1924 team played in the Rose Bowl, against Texas in the Cotton Bowl, with the national championship at stake. The Irish lost 21-17 in the final minutes, but returned the next year and ended the Longhorns' 30-game winning streak, 24-11, helped by a unique "mirror defense" that assigned man-for-man coverage on each Texas back that stopped the vaunted Wishbone offense in that game, as it did against any Wishbone opponent the Irish ever played.

Notre Dame and top-ranked Alabama played for

Left: *The Irish defeated top-ranked Alabama in the 1974 Orange Bowl.*

Below: *Joe Theismann passes for a TD in the 1970 Cotton Bowl.*

the national championship in the 1973 Sugar Bowl, and here, Parseghian endeared himself forever to Notre Dame fans still not hung up on the Michigan State tie with a thrilling 24-23 victory. The lead changed hands six times, until Bob Thomas' 19-yard field goal with 4:26 to play got the final points.

In this game, Parseghian showed his true mettle as a competitor and coach. An Alabama punt was blown dead on Notre Dame's one-yard line with three minutes to play, and Alabama coach Bear Bryant declined a penalty that would have given him another fourth-down play, hoping to force an Irish turnover deep in their territory or get a return punt with good field position. A couple of minutes later, Parseghian faced a third down inside the ten-yard line, called time out, and ordered quarterback Tom Clements to throw a pass to tight end Robin Weber. With Alabama expecting the Irish to try and wedge the ball out for punting room, the play took them by surprise and gained 31 yards, allowing the Irish to keep the ball, run out the clock and win the national title.

By that time, Parseghian had begun to be haunted by the "Ghost of Rockne," that inevitably wears down every Notre Dame head coach. Once, when he came upon a gold-plated bust of Rockne in the Athletic and Convocation Center, he stopped and looked long and hard at it.

"You," he said to the statue. "You started all this."

"I wasn't aware of Knute Rockne, Frank Leahy and all the traditions that go with the job or

Left: *Parseghian never could defeat the expectations of constant victory that was part of the coaching legacy at Notre Dame.*

Above: *Parseghian taught the Irish offense the art of the forward pass, as shown against Army in 1966.*

the magnitude of Notre Dame on a national scale," he said. "Much of the pressure is self-inflicted because there is a tradition and a sense of responsibility coaching at Notre Dame. You can't escape it and it begins to eat you up."

Indeed, Parseghian's health began to suffer as he tried to meet unwarranted expectations each year for a perfect season – not from the administration but simply because it was Notre Dame – and agonized that many scoffed at a 9-2 record. He decided to leave after the 1974 season, and his final game was against revenge-minded and second-ranked Alabama in the Orange Bowl.

Notre Dame jumped out to a 13-0 lead in the first half, and Parseghian went out as he wanted – a winner in a 13-11 decision that wasn't settled until the final two minutes, when a Notre Dame interception stopped a last Alabama drive.

Rockne and Leahy would have loved it.

JOE PATERNO

Record:

Penn State (1966-89) 220-57-3*

*Still active

With Joe Paterno, what you see is what you get, and what Penn State football has gotten during college football's most turbulent period in history is a man who has preached excellence away from the playing field and practiced it on the playing field in a way that has simply confounded his critics, and often astounded his admirers.

Unlike so many head coaches who make football the pre-eminent part of their lives, Paterno is a re-naissance man who tells his players when the season ends to join the camera club, or the dramatic society, or to go to a museum or take in lectures on anthropology, so they will have a more rounded college experience. His teams, on the other hand, reflect a "Plain Jane" philosophy that is built around a single objective: performance. For all of his erudition, his teams are never fancy, because Paterno believes the best way is the straight-forward way – no frills, no run-and-shoot, no gimmickry. This philosophy extends from the Xs and Os all the way down to his team's uniforms – dark blue jerseys with white numerals, white pants, white helmets with a single blue stripe, and black – always black – shoes, which are the same as the Nittany Lions wore when he came to Penn State in 1950 as an assistant coach to Rip Engle, for whom he had played quarterback at Brown University in the late 1940s.

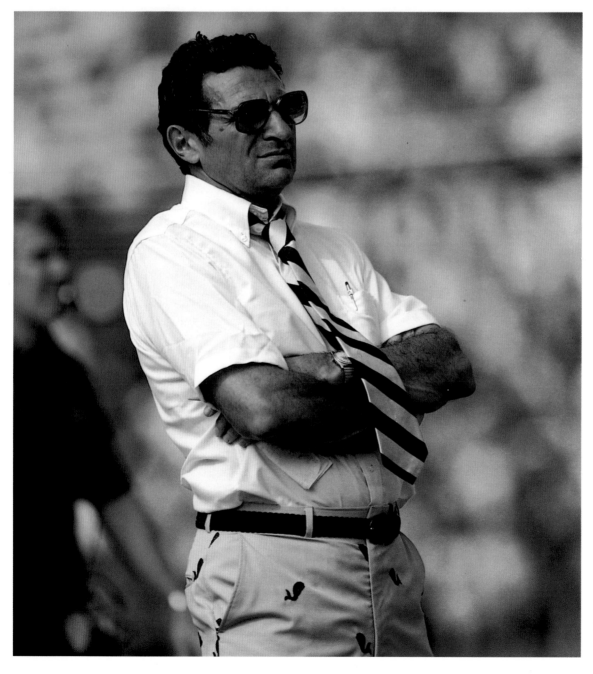

Left: *As the 1990s begin, Joe Paterno has won more games than any other active Division 1-A coach. He won a pair of national titles during the 1980s.*

Above: *Paterno and his teams are known for their "plain" look, but Paterno is also determined to have them do the things which he knows will make them successful. "I'm not as good as a lot of people paint me, nor as bad as others might say," he has said.*

Right: *Paterno was a quarterback and defensive back at Brown University under Rip Engle, who later invited him to join his staff at Penn State. He has been there ever since.*

This plain vanilla approach often becomes a point of interest for those who have nothing else to criticize – not when his teams have won 220 games, making him the winningest active Division 1-A coach entering the last decade of the century, and the sixth winningest Division 1-A coach of all time. Those victories have brought a pair of national championships in the 1980s, 19 bowl appearances, and almost a dozen Eastern titles. Every Penn State player who completed his football eligibility in the 1980s either played in an undefeated, untied season, participated in a bowl game for the national championship, or played on a team that won the national championship.

But such glory-mongering doesn't fit the Paterno persona, because he won't allow it. Instead, Paterno professes to have more pride in the fact that 85 percent of his players have graduated, numbers which are annually among the top five Division 1-A leaders.

He openly seeks players who not only have the talent to compete in the classroom, but also have the intelligence and great physical skills to produce on the playing field. He long ago realized that the player with smarts and the ability to apply himself in his studies also is largely an error-free player on the field, and one who fully understands the team concept of football and the importance of accepting and playing specific roles.

Once these players are assembled, Coach Paterno also becomes Professor Paterno, and molds that young talent into a team that wears his distinct emblem. The "plain vanilla" look that dresses his teams is also one that has made them – and him – so successful. A former Penn State linebacker, Trey Bauer, observed that Paterno appeared to "take away your individuality, but that was seen through the eyes of people not yet mature. In fact, he knew that for us to win, we had to follow his set of rules and his way of doing things. He insisted on it, we followed, and in the end, of course, he was absolutely correct, so much so that I don't think he's too far from being a saint."

Indeed, some cynics in his own profession have called him "St. Joe," but he is outwardly oblivious to this, and stands by his record as proof. "I'm bullheaded and quick-tempered, and also impatient and maybe condescending at times," he admits, "but I don't want to be a phoney, or a hypocrite. I've never had any delusions about myself, the good part and the bad part. I'm not as good as a lot of people paint me, nor as bad as others might say."

Left: *Penn State had its first perfect season ever in 1968 and won the Lambert Trophy in only Paterno's third season as head coach. Presenting the trophy to Paterno is Victor Lambert.*

Below: *The Nittany Lions, here at practice for their Sugar Bowl game against Number-1-ranked Georgia in 1983, won their first national title with a 27-23 victory over the Bulldogs to cap an 11-1 season.*

Opposite top:
Paterno's Nittany Lions matched offense with Georgia, led by Herschel Walker, in the 1983 Sugar Bowl and came up with key passes to set up their touchdowns.

Opposite bottom:
Critics said that Paterno could not win a national title, but his players give him a victory ride after his team's win in the 1983 Sugar Bowl clinched the national championship.

Above: *John Cappelletti (22) was Penn State's first Heisman Trophy winner in 1973, and was one of many great running backs who have played for Paterno.*

Never giving an inch in his insistence to do things the "right way," he follows a set of rules which rarely brook an exception. Mess up and you pay, and that is regardless of team status. In the 1972 Cotton Bowl game against Texas, he did not allow his big fullback Franco Harris to start the game because of his perceived indifference to matters of football; and he was totally unmoved when Harris' brother, Pete, an All-America safety, was declared academically ineligible before the 1977 season. "He was a goof-off in high school, and he was a goof-off here," Paterno said in his usual blunt manner. "What could I do about it? I don't care whose brother he is."

He has sent players home from bowl trips for breaking team rules, and on several occasions, he has benched starting players whose absence undoubtedly cost him games. He encourages lively discussion among his assistants, some of it reaching the high-decibel level. "Football can be an intellectual exercise," he says, "and I want people who will think about what we can do, and not be content to rubber-stamp my thoughts or be satisfied with what has worked in the past."

Paterno has consistently concocted successful game plans for important games. In the 1986 Fiesta Bowl, he outcoached Jimmy Johnson, his rival from the University of Miami, for the national championship, because Miami never fathomed a three-man pass rush and eight defenders working against its great passing game. Paterno came away with his second national title.

This is a good example of Paterno's reliance on great defense to win games, and one reason why his program has earned the nickname "Linebacker U." A dozen of his college linebackers have excelled at the position in professional football, mainly because they survived rigid training under Paterno's direction.

"It is not just the position," he said, "but a total effort by everyone who plays defense at Penn State. This is where discipline pays off, because one player who breaks down, or fails to do his job, can cost his team a victory. We put a premium on discipline on defense, because that is the only way it can be played."

The same premium on discipline is placed on offense, where Paterno's critics often get frustrated at a very conservative style of play. Yet, he always has an excellent running back – Lydell Mitchell, Harris, Curt Warner, Blair Thomas – to key his offense, and his quarterbacks mix in enough passing to give the offense a well-rounded look. They must be mistake-free, but not necessarily the team's greatest players.

Yet, his reliance on straight-ahead football probably cost him the 1978 national championship, when his fourth-and-one dive play, against a bunched-up

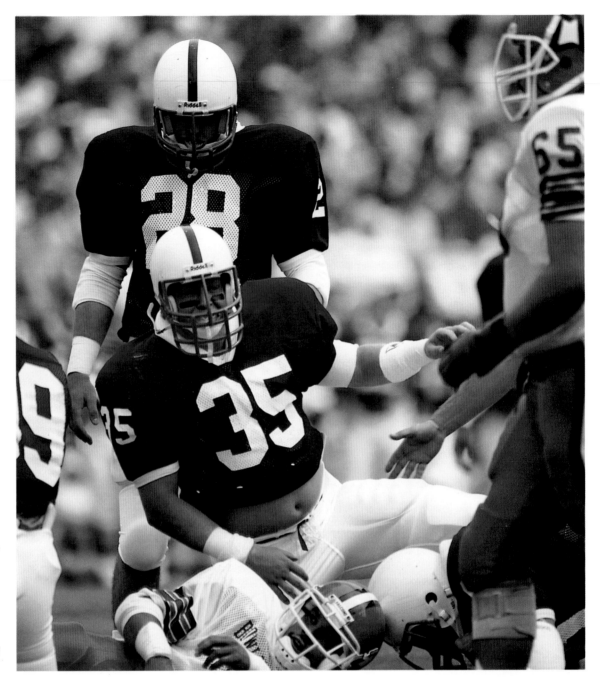

Right: *Paterno established Penn State's defense to the point where it is now known as "Linebacker U." Trey Bauer (35) was a fine linebacker for the Nittany Lions, who have sent more than a dozen to the NFL during Paterno's tenure.*

Alabama goal line defense in the waning moments of the Sugar Bowl, was stopped. His quarterback could have faked a handoff and almost strolled around end and into the end zone.

While Paterno may be single-minded in his technical approach to the game, he is not without a capacity to change. As the 1980s progressed, his offense offered more variety – where the situation was warranted – and he continued to win.

Many have preferred to look past Joe Paterno, the football coach, and dwell instead on Joe Paterno, the provocateur of education. Even his late mother, less than thrilled with her oldest son's career choice, often advised him to get "a real job," underscoring her insistence throughout his youth that he aspire to excellence. His family said she was the most powerful influence on her son, and ultimately took great pride in his achievements.

But Paterno the Coach never could be separated from Paterno the Educator, because of his love for his university. He served as vice chairman of a $200-million fund-raising campaign to which he personally donated $150,000 – $50,000 for minority scholarships and $100,000 for the library.

His own growth as a coach began after his first season in 1966, when he finished with a 5-5 record. The following season, he locked himself in a room and vowed not to fail. Then he did something about it – redesigning his defensive schemes that led to an 8-2-1 season in 1967, then back-to-back 11-0 records the next two years. It took him until 1982 to win his first national title, and he got his second in 1986. But long before those achievements, he had already proven himself a winner without peer in his obligation to make those who worked under him the best.

EDDIE ROBINSON

Record:

Grambling (1941-42)

(1945-89) 358-125-25*

*Still active

When the 1989 college football season began, Eddie Robinson cherished two distinctions: he was the only head coach in the country who was a great-grandfather; and he had won more games than any coach in history. Robinson has been head coach at Grambling State University since 1941, and in 1985, he became the game's winningest coach, breaking Bear Bryant's record of 325 wins.

Robinson's story in college football is indeed amazing, if for no other reason than for his longevity at one school. He began coaching in 1941 at what was then the Louisiana Negro Normal and Industrial Institute in Grambling, Louisiana, and even when he closed in on his 70th birthday, he steadfastly refused to discuss retirement.

His career also transcends wins and losses, because anyone who sticks around that long is bound to win a lot of games. More importantly, Robinson, while never losing sight of the need to win, has established a priority list of perspectives, of which winning games is just one entry. He can do that because there is no denying his success and ability. More than 300 of his former players went on to play professional football, and two of them, Willie Davis and Willie Brown, are enshrined in the Hall of Fame. His team is as well-known nationally and internationaly as Notre Dame, and it has played in major cities all over the country, and in some abroad, as well. He has had 27 consecutive winning seasons, the string being broken in 1988 with a 5-6 mark, two of those losses coming on bizarre plays after time had run out; and 14 Southwestern Athletic Conference titles. His team also has been named National Black Champions five times.

So much for the ledger.

The beauty of Eddie Robinson was his ability to achieve a dream that was born one day while he was in the third grade in Baton Rouge, Louisiana when Julius Kraft, the local high school football coach, brought his uniformed team to visit Eddie's school, hoping to sell 25-cent season tickets. While other third graders were enthralled with the players, Robinson couldn't take his eyes off the coach.

"I liked him from the beginning," Robinson says. "I liked the way he talked to the team, the way he could make us all laugh. I liked the way the team was dressed, in blue and white. I saw the way they all respected him."

That coach really made Eddie's day when he walked up to him, placed a hand on his head, and said, "You ought to be a good football player."

"From that moment, I knew I wanted to be a football player, to play for him, but most of all, I knew I wanted to become a football coach," he added.

A few years later Robinson joined the high school football team. And while Kraft taught Robinson some rudimentary coaching skills, more importantly he watched as Eddie, the son of share-cropper parents, became the first member of his family to graduate from high school. Robinson then played quarterback at Leland College, now defunct, in Baker, Louisiana, and his coach there, Reuben S. Turner, introduced him to the playbook

Below: *Eddie Robinson has won more games than any college coach in history, and began his sixth decade of coaching at Grambling in 1990. Only Amos Alonzo Stagg had more longevity.*

Right: *Robinson (middle) sent some great players to pro football. From left, wide receivers Frank Lewis, Sammie White and Charley Joiner were stars in the 1970s and 1980s. Jim Brown, who did not play for Robinson, is at right.*

Right: *Quarterback Doug Williams was the best quarterback ever to play for Robinson at Grambling, and later had a splendid career in the NFL, helping Washington to win Super Bowl XXII.*

and took him to his first clinic. "He brought the football world to me," Robinson says, "and taught me how to succeed in it."

Success wasn't instantaneous by any means. Robinson married his high school sweetheart, Doris, but with no coaching jobs available, he took a job in a feed mill in Baton Rouge, earning 25 cents an hour until his wife's aunt, who was attending a workshop at what now is Grambling, learned of an opening for head football coach.

Robinson convinced the school's president, Dr. Ralph Waldo Emerson Jones, who also was its band director and baseball coach, to hire him. "I had never coached before, and didn't know what you needed to do," Robinson said. "I just wanted to work hard and be the best I could be."

His first team, in 1941, had a 3-5 record, but Robinson learned quickly, and ridding himself of malingerers, he went unbeaten and unscored upon in eight games the following season. The program was stopped for two years during World War II, but Robinson logged a 10-2 record in 1945, and though he had no idea at the time, he was off in pursuit of college football's most treasured record – most victories – then at 315 and held by Amos Alonzo Stagg, another former great-grandfather head coach. Robinson eventually survived the great buildup that preceded its breaking, and long before Bryant broke Stagg's record, the two had established a close rapport.

"I would try and talk about 'the record,' with

Coach Bryant, and all he would want to talk about was his tough schedule," Robinson said. "He gave me an inkling of what it would be like."

There was more to Robinson's job than wins and losses. He mowed and lined the field by himself before the game, directed a girls' drill team at half-time, and wrote the game story and sent it to area newspapers afterward. He did most of the coaching himself, often with just a volunteer assistant or two. For many of his years at Grambling, there was little or no money, inadequate facilities (the school opened Robinson Stadium, which seats 20,000, in 1983) and little new equipment. Robinson often depended on Joe Aillet, a legendary coach at Louisiana Tech, to send him discarded equipment. In

the early years, his team's uniforms were hardly even uniforms – they often were multi-colored, because they were hand-me-downs from wherever he could obtain them.

Somehow, though, he managed to turn his program into a great training ground for future professional players, beginning with Paul (Tank) Younger, a fine fullback and linebacker with the great Los Angeles Rams teams of the late 1940s and early 1950s. Younger began a treasured tradition at Grambling, which Robinson and his players call "coming back to pay your dues," by becoming the first of many football alumni to return to the school and share his success story and offer advice to the players. When a former player comes onto

Left: *Robinson would rather coach players at Grambling, although he has had offers to coach in the NFL. "I don't ever let them forget who they are, don't ever let them forget the people who wore the Black and Gold before them and what they did," he says.*

Right: *Robinson never wished to be anything other than a College football coach, and he uses former players as role models for his current team. "We can do a lot of good, and that's the real importance of this work," he says.*

the field, a special whistle blows, and all the players stop practicing and go to the end zone. "That whistle signifies that a former athlete is present, that he is an important person, and that we are going to listen to him," Robinson explains.

The long roster of those former players includes defensive backs Roosevelt Taylor, who played with the Bears, Everson Walls of the Cowboys, Goldie Sellers from the Broncos, and Brown from the Raiders; linemen Ernie Ladd, a great tackle in the old AFL, Buck Buchanan, a member of Kansas City's 1970 Super Bowl titlists, and Willie Young; receivers Charley Joiner, the NFL's Number 2 all-time pass receiver, Charley Smith, Frank Lewis and Sammie White; and quarterbacks James Harris and Doug Williams.

Returning former players are respected, whether they are pro athletes or have chosen another profession. But Robinson strives at all times to keep alive the legacy and the tradition. "I believe you must sell the legacy and tradition to the team," he says. "I think our team will try harder because they're from Grambling. I don't ever let

them forget who they are, don't ever let them forget the people before them who wore the Black and Gold, and what they did and what they left for them."

Using former players as role models is just one facet of what Robinson always has considered "a higher calling than just playing football." He has long cared as much about preparing his players for successful lives as for careers in professional athletics. "I know what an impression a coach can make on young men, even on an elementary school child," he says. "We can do a lot of good, and that's the real importance of this work."

His work at Grambling was important enough for him to resist countless offers to move, including one to coach the Los Angeles Rams, despite the lure of greater riches. "At this stage of what I'd call a full life, you can have all the money in the world and still not be happy," he says. "The things the ball players say about our relationship and what it has meant to them is all the pay I need. When those guys come back and say, 'Eddie Robinson meant a lot to me' – money couldn't buy that."

KNUTE ROCKNE

Record:

Notre Dame (1918-30) 105-12-5

Knute Rockne: football coach, teacher, motivator, salesman, and a priceless part of the American experience whose name is as well known today as it was six decades ago when he was killed in an airplane crash while at the pinnacle of his popularity.

He was head coach at Notre Dame for only 13 years, yet no coach in history has ever matched his win-loss percentage of 88.1 percent. Nor has any football coach ever held a nation in the palm of his hand as Rockne did year after year while he worked his own brand of magic from the small, midwestern school that sat on the plains of northern Indiana, where he reached out and touched people who didn't even know what Notre Dame was, let alone where it was.

Sixty years after his death, no football coach at Notre Dame has ever shaken the "ghost of Rockne," because the standards of excellence and the aura of invincibility which he established have long outlived him. But then, how can anyone ever deal with someone who was legendary in life and deified thereafter?

Rockne's story is pure Americana: an immigrant youth who came with his family to the Midwest from Vass, Norway, who had never heard of Notre Dame until he sought a college that was affordable for his meager earnings gleaned from five years of work in the post office, and then graduated *magna cum laude* with a degree in chemistry, All-America honors as a 145-pound end in football and captain of both the football and track teams.

His greatest fame as a collegian, of course, came one afternoon in 1913 at West Point when he and teammate Gus Dorais introduced the forward pass as a lethal football weapon when Notre Dame defeated Army 35-13. From that moment, thanks to the notoriety from the heretofore skeptical Eastern press, Notre Dame's reputation was set; the forward pass was accepted as part of football's offense; and Rockne's name came to the fore.

Rockne hoped to coach high school football to help pay his way at St. Louis University's medical school, but when that deal fell through, Rockne stayed at Notre Dame to help his old coach, Jess Harper, and teach chemistry. Four years later, Harper resigned, and pushed Rockne as his successor. "The man I am recommending will go far beyond any success I may have enjoyed," Harper noted.

How right he was!

After a 3-1-2 start in 1918, the Irish reeled off 20 straight wins from 1919 until they were beaten by Iowa early in 1921, their only loss that season. Rockne perfected the Notre Dame Shift, or Box, by jazzing up the shift formation that Harper had learned from Amos Alonzo Stagg. Rockne did not invent a new formation, but shifted his backs from the T into a single wing, with each back travelling a prescribed distance with a different number of steps. The ball was centered as the backs moved in perfect unison, making it an awesome weapon that featured light, speedy backs. When the rulemakers legislated a one-second stop in the shift, Rockne used heavier backs – with the same effect.

"Pick the right men, teach them how to do things perfectly, and then make them practice,

Below: *Knute Rockne and the Notre Dame terrier mascot in 1924. Rockne is the best-known college football coach in history and has the game's best win-loss percentage.*

Right: *Rockne took Stagg's shift formation and developed the famous Notre Dame Shift that was a staple of his teams, featuring speed and quick movement. His greatest talent, though, was getting his team emotionally ready to play.*

Left: *Rockne trots onto the field for the first game of the 1913 season against Ohio Northern. He was captain of that Irish team that went unbeaten for the second straight season, teaming with Gus Dorais to form a great pass-catch combination.*

Below: *Rockne (middle) worked as an assistant under his old coach Jess Harper (left) for five years before becoming a head coach in 1918. He started a 22-game unbeaten streak in his first season as head coach.*

practice, practice," he said, when insisting the game was not complicated.

He found the ideal players to make it go. First, there was George Gipp, a strapping young maverick and a marvelously gifted athlete who played football with the same verve as he hustled cards and pool. Gipp, who missed Rockne's first season because of a broken leg, had the perfect athleticism for this offense, and he keyed the 20-game winning streak. Against Army in 1919, Notre Dame trailed 9-0 and was on the Cadets' one-yard line as Gipp noticed the official raising a horn to his mouth to signal the end of the first half. As the backs were about to shift, he shouted, "Give me the ball," and center O. J. Larson obliged. Gipp bulled through for a TD that led to Notre Dame's 12-9 victory. In 1920, he passed for two touchdowns and kicked three extra points in a 27-17 victory.

Just after the 1921 season ended, Gipp died of pneumonia. With Rockne at his bedside in his final moments, his star told him, "Sometime, Rock, when things are wrong and the breaks are beating the boys, tell them to go in there with all they've got and win one just for the Gipper. I don't know

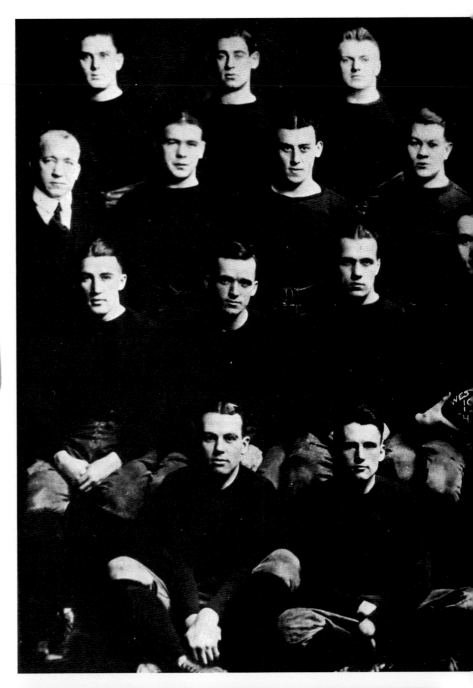

Above: *All-America back George Gipp, whose deathbed request to "win one for the Gipper" became the game's most famous pep talk.*

Right: *Notre Dame's most famous rival during Rockne's time was Army. Here, Jim Brady carries for the Irish in 1928.*

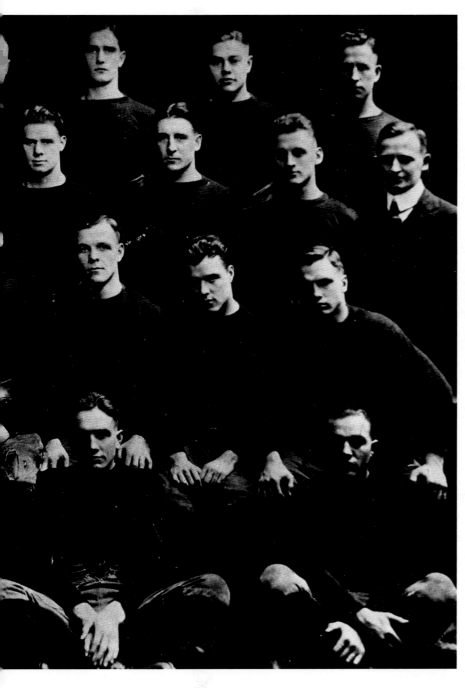

Left: *Rockne (third row, far left) and his unbeaten 1920 team with George Gipp (front row, second from right).*

Above: *Rockne was sought by many firms as a motivational speaker. He also was a prolific writer who had a nationally syndicated column.*

where I'll be then, Rock, but I'll know about it and I'll be happy."

In 1928, when Notre Dame was an underdog to Army, Rockne fulfilled that wish, telling his players in the most dramatic fashion, with his voice rising and falling, of Gipp's plea. trailing 6-0, the Irish sprung to life in the second half as Jack Chevigny shouted Gipp's name on every carry until he burst across for the first score, and cried out his memorable, "Here's one of them for you, Gipper!"

As if one bit of legend wasn't enough, Army finally was defeated that day by end Johnny (One-Play) O'Brien, who had entered the game with just two minutes to play. On the next play, the lanky end faked Red Cagle out of position, and sprinted into the right corner of the end zone where Johnny Niemiec's pass barely dropped into his outstretched arms as he tumbled to the ground. He arose, and

trotted back to the Irish bench, forever famous for that one play.

Such drama was typical of Rockne's regime at Notre Dame, where everything always seemed to be high theater. When Gipp's era ended, it was replaced by that of the Four Horsemen – Jim Crowley, Elmer Layden, Harry Stuhldreher and Don Miller. They were light, pony backs but ideal for Rockne's offense, though their effectiveness came from an offensive line nicknamed the Seven Mules. Together, they helped Rockne to a third unbeaten 1924 season, a national title and a Rose Bowl victory. Every so often, Rockne sensed that his stars were believing all the superlatives in the press, so he'd yank the Mules from a game. Naturally, the backs had problems, and he would taunt them, "See, without the Mules, you Horsemen are just turtles!"

Overleaf: *The Four Horsemen – (l to r) Don Miller, Elmer Layden, Jim Crowley and Harry Stuhldreher – were the most famous four-man backfield in the game's history and the stars of Rockne's unbeaten 1924 team that also won the Rose Bowl. The offensive line was known as the Seven Mules.*

Above: *Thousands stood outside Notre Dame's chapel during Rockne's funeral in the spring of 1931. He was killed in an airplane crash while en route to the West Coast on business for a sporting goods firm.*

The Rockne legend grew from these bits of motivation, and there was no one better in the country – coach and non-coach alike – at the art. First of all, he had believability because he was a successful coach, a perfect stylist whose system stressed speed, power, shock, and the highest deception the sport had known to that time. His teams were sound in the fundamentals of tackling and blocking. He was close to them, gave personal attention to their welfare, and then used his greatest asset – salesmanship.

Above all else, Rockne was a salesman, one so well recognized that at the time of his death he had been appointed sales director for the Studebaker Corporation, a leading auto manufacturer with headquarters in South Bend. He sold his brand of football to his players, complete with full effort, total attention, and playing above one's capacity. He did it as coach-to-player, but when necessary, with any number of well-conceived ideas – the Gipper story was just one of them. On another occasion, when his team trailed 7-0 at the half against Northwestern, he went to the locker room, told his team he was quitting, walked out and sat in the stands. When the Irish staged a comeback in the

third quarter, he returned to the bench. When his team was an underdog, he had his children's baby-sitter dispatch a telegram saying that his son, Billy, was ill in the hospital and asked the team to win for him. It did – but it was startled on arriving back in South Bend to see "sick" little Billy cavorting about. When he sensed his team was overconfident before playing Beloit, he mailed copies of every Notre Dame play to the team's coach. Notre Dame won 19-3, but regained his attention. He could play the moan-and-groan game with the best. While his 1930 team, heading for a second straight perfect season and his last national championship, prepared to play an undermanned Carnegie Tech team, he so convinced the press the Irish couldn't win that they became the underdog. When they won handily, the headline in the *New York Times* read: NOTRE DAME UPSETS CARNEGIE TECH 21-6.

He always considered his 1930 team as the best, with a backfield of Frank Carideo, Joe Savoldi, Marty Brill and Marchie Schwartz. They had also won the 1929 national title with a 9-0 record, but Rockne had battled phlebitis, attending games and giving emotional locker room talks against doctor's orders. They feared the blood clot in his leg would break loose and lodge in his brain or heart. In fact, it did break, but it passed through the heart without consequence. He had regained his health in 1930, and after a second straight national title, he was at the peak of his popularity, with his own newspaper column, supervising movie short subjects, running a football camp, making countless speeches, working for Studebaker, and becoming athletic director at Notre Dame – and still the offers poured in. One was to represent a chain of sporting good stores, so on March 31, 1931, he was in Kansas City to fly to the West Coast for some store openings.

A ticket mix-up cancelled his space, but as he turned to leave the ticket counter, another passenger recognized him and offered his own seat. Gratefully, Rockne accepted. An hour later, he was dead after the plane, its wings laden with ice, crashed into farmland near Bazaar, Kansas.

Ten thousand jammed a Chicago railroad station when his body was returned, and funeral services at Notre Dame's chapel were broadcast worldwide. Rev. John O'Donnell, Notre Dame's president, delivered the eulogy:

"Knute Rockne is dead, and who was he?

"Ask the president, who dispatched a personal message.

"Ask the King of Norway, who sends a delegation.

"Ask thousands of newspapermen.

"Ask men and women in every walk of life.

"Ask the children of America . . ."

They knew . . . and so do their children, and their children's children.

DARRELL ROYAL

Record:

Mississippi State (1954-55)	12-8-0
Washington (1956)	5-5-0
Texas (1957-76)	167-47-5

In 1956, when he was coaching at Texas A&M, someone asked Bear Bryant whether he saw any good, young future coaching stars. "There are three of them," Bryant said, "and the brightest is Darrell Royal."

Bryant rarely was mistaken about anything dealing with football during his life, and he was dead-on when he tabbed Royal as a future coaching star. At the time, Darrell had finished two seasons at Mississippi State, and had just become head coach at the University of Washington, where he would spend just one season before being hired by Texas.

Royal had come from the "dust bowl" section of Oklahoma under Bud Wilkinson. Wilkinson called him "one of the most adept T-formation quarterbacks I ever coached," and for good reason – Wilkinson's teams had won 21 of 22 games with Royal running his split-T offense, including all 11 during the 1949 season. He also had been a crack punt return specialist and the Sooners' best defensive back, who had intercepted 17 passes during his career.

Wilkinson's offense had captivated college football with its success, and many teams were anxious

to learn its secrets. North Carolina State coach Beattie Feathers struck first and hired Royal as an assistant coach, to tutor his quarterbacks and freshmen, and Royal soon made stops at Tulsa University and Mississippi State before getting his first head coaching job with the Edmonton Eskimos of the Canadian Football League. He stayed there for a year, then returned to the United States to his first collegiate head coaching job, with Mississippi State at age 29.

Three years later, his name was one of 100 prospects the University of Texas considered to replace head coach Ed Price, who had lost nine of ten games in 1956. The list was pruned to 11 "among the foremost in the country,"and Royal, despite his relative youth and limited head coaching experience, got the job.

Royal wasted no time. The Longhorns had a winning record and a bowl bid in his first season; he defeated his old coach, Wilkinson and the Longhorns' arch-rival Sooners in his second year; and won nine out of ten games in his third season to share the first of 11 Southwest Conference championships in his career.

This was when Royal first showed his talent as an innovator, first coming up with his "Flip-Flop Wing-T," allowing his backfield to flip right or left, without altering blocking assignments. It pressured defenses to play his Wing-T offense "honestly," and in a three-season period, from 1961 to 1963, the Longhorns had a 30-2-1 record. In 1961, running back James Saxton averaged more than eight yards per carry, and Royal often favorably compared that team to his 1963 team, which was

Below left: *In his playing days, Darrell Royal was one of "the most adept T-formation quarterbacks I ever coached," said his former coach, Bud Wilkinson. Royal won 21 of the 22 games he started at Oklahoma. He got his first head coaching job at age 29.*

Below: *As head coach at Texas from 1957 through 1976, Royal's major opponent for supremacy in the Southwest Conference was the University of Arkansas, which he beat for the 1969 national title.*

unbeaten and won the first of three national championships. It punctuated the season with a thundering 28-6 victory over second-ranked Navy in the Cotton Bowl.

In this game, Royal showed his flexibility by using a weapon he often dreaded: the forward pass. Despite the fact that he was one of Oklahoma's most accurate passers, his defensive backfield experience had convinced him that too many bad things happen with a team that throws the ball. Yet, against Navy and its Heisman Trophy winning quarterback Roger Staubach, Royal had his team pass more in one day than it had in his previous seven seasons, and it stunned Navy with a pair of 58- and 63-yard TD passes as part of a 213-yard passing day by quarterback Duke Carlisle.

His next innovation came in 1968 – the Wishbone, or triple option, offense – and it revolutionized college football for the next decade. The backfield alignment featured the fullback lined up two yards behind the quarterback, and the two halfbacks a yard to each side, and a yard further back. The quarterback had the option of handing the ball to the fullback going straight ahead – the key play that made the offense successful, because it forced the defense to play tighter in the middle, and opened the flanks to the quarterback who, as in the wing-T, ran along the line of scrimmage, with both backs trailing, and had the option of either keeping the ball and turning upfield when he saw an opening, or pitching it back if his backs were uncovered. The speed and deception were often frightening with a quarterback such as the Longhorns' James Street, who helped Texas to a pair of national titles in 1969 and 1970.

While some coaches, such as Bryant, added a passing capability to the Wishbone, Royal blanched at the thought until December 6, 1969, when battling Arkansas for the Number 1 spot in college football, and Texas trailed 14-0 going into the last quarter. Street ran 42 yards for a TD, then added the two-point conversion to cut the deficit to 14-8. With four minutes to play, Royal forgot his aversion to the pass and Street's 47-yard pass, on fourth-and-three, helped set up the Longhorns' winning touchdown.

Less than a month later, in the Cotton Bowl against Notre Dame, his team trailed once more late in the game, and again Street set up the winning score with a pass to the three-yard line as Texas won its second national title.

But there was more to Royal's team than speed and deception on the playing field. It was a perfect mirror of its coach, one marked by a fierce intensity of competition, without, as one coach noted, "emotional or rah-rah tactics."

"It was," another coach added, "a matter of knowing what had to be done, and keeping your head so as to be better able to accomplish it."

That was how Royal worked, both as player and coach, and later as athletic director, a post he took at age 32 while also coaching the team. Yet, he also looked at more important things, employing the nation's first academic counsellor as one of his first acts when he became head coach in 1957. Over the years, four of every five football lettermen achieved their degrees, and he so valued this element of college life that he set aside a fund for a special "T" ring which he personally awarded to his players upon their graduation.

Royal also lobbied long and hard for stricter rules to ensure the integrity of the game. "Integrity was a key word for Darrell," Neils Thompson, a past president of the NCAA noted. "He ran his football team accordingly, and lived by the rules. If he didn't like them, he would fight to change them, but he never would intentionally break them."

This style also captivated Lyndon B. Johnson, the president of the United States and a native Texan. Once after a key victory, he wrote to Royal: "You are the finest example of an inspiring leader I know." After Johnson had left the presidency and returned to his ranch in the Lone Star State, he was a regular attendee at Texas home games.

"I'm not a football fan," Johnson said, "but I am a fan of people, and I am a Darrell Royal fan because he is the rarest of human beings."

Above: *Royal (left) accepts the MacArthur Bowl after winning the 1969 national championship. With him are two of his tri-captains, James Street and Ted Koy (Glenn Halsell is not shown). Street ran Royal's famed Wishbone offense that season.*

Opposite: *Royal won eight post-season games for the Longhorns. Here he gets a victory ride after defeating Alabama 17-13 in the 1973 Cotton Bowl.*

GLENN (BO) SCHEMBECHLER

Record:

Miami (Ohio) (1963-68) 40-17-3

Michigan (1969-89) 194-48-5

Just over four minutes remained on the clock when Michigan scored a touchdown to trail Notre Dame 17-12 in the opening game of the 1989 season. This game was billed as a battle of prospective national champions, and all Michigan had to do was to kick off to the Irish, hold them and force a punt, and win the game in the final minutes. Why not? The Wolverines had the momentum and were being wildly urged on by 106,000 fans at Michigan Stadium.

At the start of the second half, Notre Dame's Raghib Ismail had returned the kickoff 88 yards for a touchdown, so as the Michigan players gathered around their coaches prior to this kickoff, the suggestion was proferred: "Don't kick the ball to Ismail."

"What do you mean, don't kick the ball to

Right: *Bo Schembechler retired after the 1989 season as the fifth winningest coach in major college football history, and with the most wins ever by a Michigan coach. He won 192 games for the Wolverines from 1969 through the 1989 season.*

Left: *Schembechler was a fiery leader on the sidelines who never allowed his teams to relax or get complacent during a game. He was unyielding and often stubborn, even if it cost him a game.*

Below: *Officials often knew enough to keep their distance lest they get scalded by Schembechler's tongue. Sometimes that got him into trouble, as happened in his final game in the 1990 Rose Bowl when a 15-yard penalty for his unsportsmanlike conduct helped Southern Cal in its winning touchdown drive. Here he is seen with quarterback Rick Leach in 1975.*

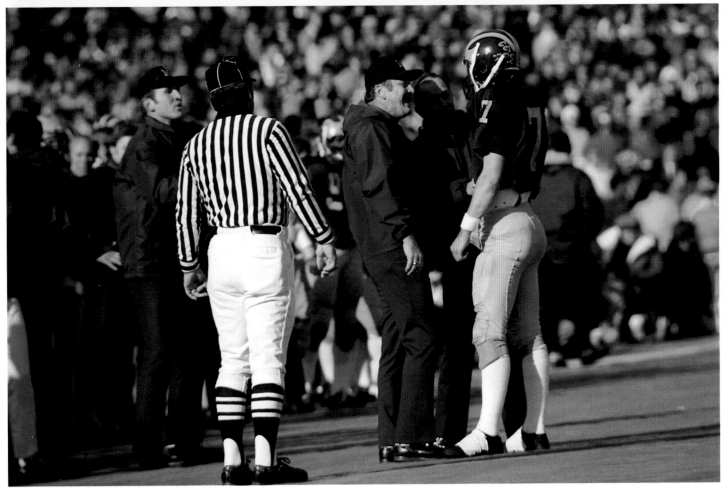

Above: *Schembechler shows QB Rick Leach his passing style while the team prepares to play the 1978 Rose Bowl game. But that part of the game was not to his liking because he was raised by his old boss, Woody Hayes, to believe that the run over the pass was the only way to win.*

Left: *Schembechler filled Michigan Stadium's 106,000 seats week after week during his 20 seasons at Ann Arbor because his teams always contended for a title. Even in rare times of so-so success, Bo's critics backed off because he was a supreme ruler in Wolverine Land.*

him?" Wolverines coach Bo Schembechler yelled. "We'll kick it to him, and then we're going to knock his ass off. He's not going to get us again. Got it?"

So Michigan kicked the ball to Ismail, and this time he returned the ball 92 yards for a game-deciding touchdown in an eventual 24-19 Notre Dame victory.

That was pure Bo Schembechler: stubborn, unyielding, determined to succeed in his way, and if you don't like it, find another ball and go play with someone else.

That "pure" Bo Schembechler is also one reason why, at his retirement after the 1989 season, he was the fifth winningest coach in Division 1-A history, with 234 victories. His stubbornness was wrapped tightly around an equally firm will that always strove for perfection, and drove those around him toward the same end. It was also the basis of a love-hate relationship he "enjoyed" with Michigan alumni and fans, and a running battle with media critics who too often gleefully presented only his fiery and stubborn side and ignored the other qualities which made him successful.

There were no shortcuts in Schembechler's coaching style. Some, including his good friend and former Michigan All-America center, Gerald Ford, the 38th president of the United States, say that he mellowed somewhat following two heart opera-

tions. "Frankly, I think he's a more effective coach when he's less tense," the former president said.

Schembechler always denied that he changed, and his insistence on team play over individual stardom and a constant work ethic that demanded that everyone – including himself – improve every day was as strong in his last year as a head coach as it was when he began as a head coach in 1963 at Miami University in Oxford, Ohio. "I may want a better player, but I can't trade for one or pick up one as a free agent," he said. "So I'll coach the hell out of the guy because he has to play – and because he's mine."

A former defensive coach, Bill McCartney, said, "Nobody calls to excellence more than he does. He forces every guy to measure up every time. He will never turn his head."

In 1975, for example, after the Wolverines were stunned in a tie against Baylor, Schembechler called in his equipment manager, Jon Falk, and asked why one of the Michigan linemen had a wrinkled number on his jersey.

"I didn't think you would notice," said Falk.

"I notice everything," Schembechler said. "Now if you want to manage the goddamn equipment, get busy and manage the goddamn equipment."

This all had its beginnings in Barberton, Ohio and later at Miami of Ohio, where he played offensive

Below: *Quarterback Jim Harbaugh was a deft ball handler who became a Number 1 draft pick of the Chicago Bears despite only average throwing ability. Bo always stressed athleticism and mobility with his quarterbacks to fit his offense of run first and throw only if absolutely necessary.*

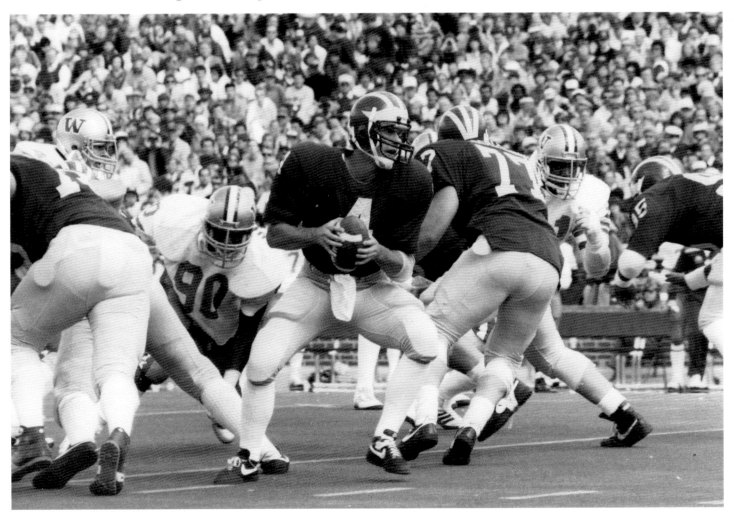

Above: *Schembechler and his old boss, Woody Hayes of Ohio State, two very emotional people whose discussions sometimes ended in chair-throwing sessions. Their friendship never suffered, even though the schools are fierce rivals.*

tackle under Woody Hayes for whom he later worked, first as a graduate assistant and later for five years as a line coach before becoming head coach at Michigan.

His relationship with Hayes was as interesting as it was close. Both were very strong persons, and while Schembechler always deferred to Hayes as his boss and his "old head coach," it wasn't without some fire and brimstone, including an instance or two when the disagreements reached the chair-throwing stage. Still, they remained the closest of friends until Hayes' death, even through an intense 10-year rivalry, since the Michigan-Ohio State game always seemed to decide the Big Ten championship. Bo led 5-4-1.

It was no accident that Schembechler was called "little Woody," because their personal styles were so similar. Hayes was renowned for his temper and sideline histrionics, and so was Schembechler. This carried over to the practice field as well, and he made no apologies.

"I know I've got a lousy temper, but sometimes it can make a player compete better," he said. "But I'm smart enough to know you have to control it. It's just when things aren't right. I react aggressively and I'm a disciplinarian. At meetings,

players sit up straight, have both feet on the floor and don't wear any hats. They get in early at night, too. I guess my philosophy is that I want to do what I'm doing better than anyone else."

He did it at every turn. He took films away on vacation with his wife, Millie, "just in case it is raining and we can't go out." Even if it didn't rain, he managed to watch them. Once, on the night before a game against woeful Northwestern, his film-watching convinced him that "Northwestern is good and we aren't ready," whereupon, as someone noted, he "went on a rampage through the hotel, clicking off TVs, screaming, berating, threatening, kicking ass and taking names." The next day, Michigan won 69-0.

He became famous for such outbursts, and was made a caricature of sorts by the media, who loved his outbursts because they made good copy and dynamic sound bytes, and because they didn't have to ask him questions that could bring their own knowledge into question, and with it, the sting of the Schembechler tongue. The one area where he was constantly criticized, even when his teams were successful, was in a perceived indifference (some say fear) regarding the use of the passing game. Perhaps because so much was made of his

Below: *A player had to have drive and enthusiasm to play for Schembechler, if only to match his coach's feelings for the game. Tight end Eric Kattus, who played in the NFL for the Cincinnati Bengals, lets it all go after scoring a TD for the Wolverines.*

Right: *Critics always said that Schembechler couldn't win bowl games, but he always felt the true test was winning the Big Ten championship. Here, he gets a ride atop his players' shoulders after winning Fiesta Bowl XV against Nebraska.*

Above: *Schembechler never had much success in the Rose Bowl, losing nine of the ten times he played there. His 1982 team got the only victory as it defeated UCLA.*

conservative philosophy, there was a feeling that every time a Michigan quarterback dropped back to pass, Schembechler wished he was some place else. The criticism had two roots, one being the Wolverines' inability to win post-season games consistently against opponents who threw the ball without timidity, and the other being the influence of Hayes, who, as noted earlier, had an aversion to the pass, which he conveyed to his star pupil.

Perhaps because of his stubbornness, Schembechler ignored the critics – but his teams always included at least one great receiver. However, he always held fast to his prime commandment: "You run the ball first, and if you are successful, you keep running it." When Bo passed, whether it be to shake up a defense, or, as he did in the last moments of the second game of the 1989 season against UCLA, to win, there was not the least concession that maybe the passing game had equal standing with the running game.

"There are coaches who say that every time we beat them, we always did it with the pass," Schembechler has pointed out. "I think because we do run the ball, and we've been 1-2-3 in the conference, and in the top ten nationally in rushing stats, everyone assumes that it's predominantly rush at Michigan. It's no different with teams that the media feel are passing teams: When we've lost to them, it's been their running game that has beaten us. You must be able to do both, and if you

can't, then you can't win."

While Schembechler existed happily with his own offensive ideas, he was successful because of how he coached his team. He had a firm view on everything, and his decision-making was always aggressive. He didn't sleep on decisions, and he rarely was wrong, which is one big reason why he never had a losing season; is the winningest coach in Michigan history; took his Michigan teams to 17 bowl games in 21 seasons, including 15 in a row through 1989; and accumulated 13 Big Ten titles or co-championships, with an .838 conference winning percentage.

He emphasized Big Ten titles over national championships, though 17 of his Michigan teams were ranked in the top ten, but none ever finished Number 1. "Our goal is to win the Big Ten Championship," he said. "If we win the Big Ten and the Rose Bowl, that's a great season. Now, if they want to vote us Number 1, I'll go up there and accept the trophy. But that's not what I'm playing for."

He loved nothing more than to win, but insisted that his program be run honestly. There was never a hint of any recruiting irregularities under his regime. "When I'm through coaching, they're going to say that Bo Schembechler was an old, hard-nosed bastard, a pretty good coach. But he was honest and you could believe what he said. That's good enough, I don't need anything else."

FLOYD (BEN) SCHWARTZWALDER

Record:
Muhlenberg (1946-48) 25-5-0
Syracuse (1949-73)   153-91-3

Jim Brown; Ernie Davis; Jim Nance; Floyd Little; Larry Csonka. Not a bad group of running backs, and any coach would feel pretty fortunate just to have had one of them during his career. If that is the case, Floyd (Ben) Schwartzwalder must have soared through a good part of his coaching career at Syracuse riding on Cloud Nine, because he coached them all.

All but Davis, who won the Heisman Trophy in 1961 and died tragically two years later from leukemia, had great NFL careers and received as much, if not more, notoriety at that level than from playing college football. But Schwartzwalder made the best possible use of them – his teams outrushed opponents by more than 22,000 yards – to win one national championship (1959, with Davis), four Lambert Trophies (1956, with Brown; 1959, with Davis; 1964, with Little; and 1966, with Csonka); make five of his seven bowl appearances; get 14 of his 22 consecutive non-losing seasons; and 98 of his 153 victories with the Orange.

Schwartzwalder's insistence on using a big running back intelligently speaks volumes about his successful career. He actively sought the big back because he believed that a run-oriented, inside offense was more effective than one that spread the ball to all parts of the field. With Brown, Davis and Little, he had backs who could run inside *and* outside, and he didn't tie them down. His running backs were always the stars of his team, not his quarterbacks, and Schwartzwalder made certain that they operated behind huge offensive lines with All-America players such as Roger Davis, Maury Youmans, Fred Mautino, Ron Luciano (later an American League umpire), and Bob Yates.

He made his first big splash just three years after becoming the school's fourth head coach in five seasons when his 1952 team won the Eastern title and went to the Orange Bowl, its first post-season trip ever. The game, however, was a nightmare, because a tight, error-free team for nine games suddenly fell apart, as six of Pat Stark's passes were intercepted by Alabama in a 61-6 rout. From that point on, Schwartzwalder decided that he never again would have to rely on a passing game, and two years later, he had recruited Jim Brown, who became the greatest athlete ever at Syracuse – he was also an All-America lacrosse player and a varsity letter winner in basketball and boxing.

Brown really didn't develop into arguably the greatest running back in history until his years with the Cleveland Browns of the NFL, but during three varsity seasons at Syracuse he reflected Schwartzwalder's philosophy that "when a team lines up against its equal, basic fundamentals pay off . . . you don't ever beat a good football team just by fooling it." In other words, if you have a big gun, you keep firing it until it either runs out of ammunition or the enemy is destroyed.

Brown led the 1956 Orangemen to an 8-1 record, and came within kicking distance of an extra point which would get them a tie in the Cotton Bowl against TCU. He scored three of Syracuse's touchdowns, kicked three extra points and saw the potential tie-maker blocked in the final minutes.

Davis continued the same excellence as Syracuse went unbeaten in 1959 and was declared national champion. Though Schwartzwalder always had a reputation as being a hard-bitten, rather crusty old coach, he had a genuine affection for Davis. In all his 25 years as a college football coach, Schwartzwalder said he never met another player like him.

"He had spontaneous goodness about him, he

Below: *Floyd (Ben) Schwartzwalder was a no-nonsense coach who believed in driving a ball right down the throat of an opponent, and he always built his teams around big, powerful backs.*

radiated enthusiasm," Schwartzwalder said. "He'd knock a guy down on the field, and when the play ended, he'd run back and help him up. He patted tacklers on the back and congratulated them for a good hit. Some of them even came into our dressing room after the game to see him.

"It was different with Brown, Little and Csonka," he added. "They would knock a guy down, or run over him because they just didn't like anyone with a different color uniform during the game. They were the enemy."

Schwartzwalder also didn't mind that feeling, because that is how he believed football should be played, the way he had learned it as a 155-pound center at West Virginia under Earle (Greasy) Neale in the early 1930s. It was also the way he found life in combat as a 35-year-old paratroop officer with the 82nd Airborne Division during World War II when he won the Silver Star, Bronze Star, Purple Heart, four battle stars, and a Presi-

dential Unit Citation for heroism during the D-Day invasion of Europe in 1944.

Prior to the war, he had been a successful high school coach in West Virginia, and had won an appointment as head coach of McKinley High School in Canton, Ohio, one of the best coaching jobs in Ohio before the war intervened. When the war was over, he went to Muhlenberg College in Pennsylvania for three years before going to Syracuse, then known as a "graveyard of coaches" because of such a rapid post-war turnover. At first he turned down the job, but changed his mind after he was assured the school was willing to make the necessary investment to maintain a sound athletic program.

His unbeaten 1959 team, which defeated Texas in the Cotton Bowl, 23-14, was his best team. It led the nation in total offense, rushing offense, and scoring average, and underlined his belief that a team had to be strong defensively by topping the

Below: *Jim Brown was the first of a series of great backs to play for Schwartzwalder at Syracuse. He once scored a record 44 points in one game and later became the greatest running back in NFL history.*

Left: *Schwartzwalder and the last of his great backs, Larry Csonka, who went on to lead the Miami Dolphins to a pair of NFL championships. He followed in the footsteps of Jim Brown, 1961 Heisman Trophy winner Ernie Davis, Jim Nance and Floyd Little.*

nation in total defense, allowing just 93 yards per game and only 19.3 yards per game rushing. At the end of that season, his team was the only major unbeaten and untied team in the country, and he was named Coach of the Year.

The public Ben Schwartzwalder has often appeared to be a cross between a wounded bear and a crossed bull. He was basically a shy person, quiet except in the company of close friends, and he never cared to get very close to the press or general public. But his real self was probably best amplified when, as he was finishing his tenure as president of the American Football Coaches Association, he told his fellow coaches:

"We football coaches are most fortunate. By doing the best we can with the job we have, wherever it is, we can serve our nation in its greatest task – the making of healthy, useful citizens of the raw material that is the youth of today."

That was the real Ben Schwartzwalder.

AMOS ALONZO STAGG

Record:

Springfield College (1890-91)	10-11-1
Univ. of Chicago (1892-1932)	244-111-27
College of the Pacific (1933-46)	60-77-7

Below: Amos Alonzo Stagg, the Father of American Football, is the third winningest coach in the game's history and its foremost innovator. His new offensive ideas helped to develop the game from its rudimentary stages in the late nineteenth century.

Amos Alonzo Stagg is to college football what Benjamin Franklin, Thomas Alva Edison and Alexander Graham Bell were to the Eras of Discovery.

The key parts of the game as it is played today all had roots in the fertile imagination of "The Grand Old Man," and to him must go the credit for developing the sport into the grand spectacle which makes it Number 1 among America's sporting preferences. And while he was at it, he also managed to become the third biggest winner in the game's history with 314 victories, a feat that stood above

all others until Bear Bryant, and later, Eddie Robinson, finally surpassed it during the 1980s, nearly two decades after his death in 1965 at the grand old age of 102.

Stagg's career must be viewed through bifocals, to appreciate both his excellence as an innovator and as a coach dealing with people. Stagg inventions are now basic to the sport:

T-formation QB	Jersey Numbers
Pitchouts	Formation Shifts
Onside Kick	Cross Blocking
Intersectional Play	Wind Sprints
Direct Center Snap	Reverses
Man in Motion	Spiral Punt
Indoor Football	Running Pass
Lit Practice Field	QB Keeper
Men in Motion	Lateral Pass
Tackling Dummy	Knit FB Pants
Pulling Linemen	Cut Back Run
Varsity Letters	Flankers

Not bad for a lifetime's work, but he conceived and implemented all of them by 1918, when he had already coached 28 years – and another three decades lay ahead of him!

Stagg coined the term "pigskin," because he used the bladders from slaughtered pigs to play football during his youth in East Orange, New Jersey. He was also involved with other sports. He helped Dr. James Naismith, a 30-year old center on his first football team at the School of Christian Workers (later Springfield YMCA College) in Massachusetts, with the development of the game of basketball, and scored the only point through that famed peach basket for the school's faculty in a 5-1 loss to Naismith's students in the first game ever played. He invented the spillway trough that runs around a swimming pool; borrowed money for the only time in his life to help send four University of Chicago trackmen to the 1904 Olympic Games in Paris, where his protege, James Goodbody, won three medals; arranged the first trip to the Far East by an American baseball team; and invented the indoor baseball batting cage, partly as the result of his own experience as a star pitcher for Yale when he led the Eli to five straight championships, then turned down a major league contract from the New York Nationals.

Stagg revelled in his work, and he expected all under him to hold to his very rigid ideas. He treated his players as if they were sons, but was very demanding and precise on the field. He could be acerbic to fire someone up, or he could put an arm

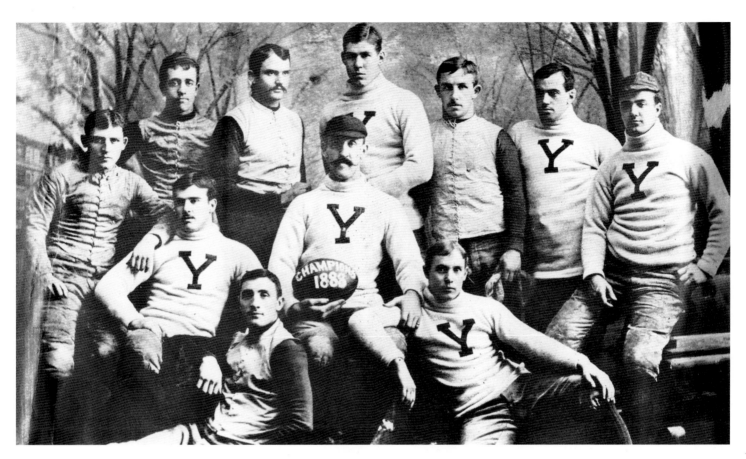

around a shoulder, walk a young player over the field and, pointing out where one of his great players had once made a big play, tell him he could do the same. He rewarded them with ice cream after victories at Chicago; and at College of the Pacific, with a dish of fresh figs. "Get acquainted" sessions at his home were "spiced" with soft drinks and cookies.

Stagg didn't drink, smoke, or use profanity. His strongest expletive was "jackass" and if matters got serious, "double jackass," or "triple jackass," and on a rare occasion, someone was declared "king of the jackasses." When someone once pointed out to Bob Zuppke, the Illinois coach, that Stagg didn't swear, he noted, "Maybe so, but by the end of each practice, a team of jackasses is grazing on the field."

Stagg was as renowned for his principles as he was for his innovations, and he never hesitated to bench star players who broke training rules – one even got benched for continually humming off-color ditties. He was also known for his sense of fair play. When the referee in a game between Illinois and Chicago was injured, Stagg was asked to replace the official, and referee his own game. After losing a game to Ohio State on a blatantly bad call by an official, Stagg was asked if he was disturbed. "Yes, I am a little disturbed," he said in his very quiet manner. "I've misplaced my topcoat and Mrs. Stagg will be furious."

"Mrs. Stagg" was always a very special part of his life. He married Stella Robertson, a 19-year-old

Above: *Stagg (far left) was a member of the 1888 Yale team that won 13 games and scored 698 points without allowing any. The team also included Pa Corbin (with ball) and Pudge Heffelfinger (third from left, back row), both Hall of Famers.*

Left: *Stagg coached at Springfield YMCA College after he graduated from Yale and worked with Dr. James Naismith in developing the game of basketball.*

Overleaf: *Stagg, shown addressing his University of Chicago team in 1930, won 244 games for the school between 1892 and 1932, when it was one of the Big Ten's early powerhouses.*

Above: *Stagg was a hands-on coach and sometimes scrimmaged with his team. Here he holds the ball for University of Chicago kicker Don Birney.*

coed at Chicago, and delayed their honeymoon until after the 1894 season, when his team was invited to play Stanford on the West Coast, in the first intersectional game ever played. The new bride – and 22 players – all went West on the honeymoon. Mrs. Stagg soon became her husband's football alter ego, scouting opponents, and was the one person Stagg relied on for accurate spotter's information during games.

Stagg got into coaching by accident after graduating from Yale, where he was selected to Walter Camp's All-America team in 1889 as a 150-pound end. He aspired to the ministry when he joined the faculty of the Christian Workers School, and got his first football coaching job there. He played for two years and captained the team, as he did on his first teams at the University of Chicago. He scrimmaged with his players well into his forties, played tennis into his eighties, and jogged each day until he was 96.

William Rainey Harper, a former professor of Stagg's at Yale and newly-appointed president of the new University of Chicago, invited his former pupil to become the school's first football coach in 1892 for $2500 a year and tenure as a professor. Still wrestling with his ministry career, Stagg requested more time to consider it, then wrote Harper, "After much thought and prayer, I have decided that my life can best be used for my Master's service in the position you have offered."

Stagg didn't even have a stadium, but collected $866 from students and faculty, hired a carpenter and got enough free student help to build a makeshift field, later improved to become the famed Stagg Field, under which scientists did much of the development for the atomic bomb during World War II when the school no longer played football.

He wasted no time becoming an outstanding coach, helped by his own innovations. In 41 years, from 1892 until 1932, five of his teams were unbeaten and seven of them won Western Conference (Big Ten) titles. The 1905 team scored 272 points and allowed only five, winning its final game of the season, 2-0, over Fielding Yost's great Michigan team, which was unbeaten in 56 straight games. The game was scoreless at the half, with President Harper, bedridden and slowly dying of cancer, listening on a special phone hookup. He sent a message to Stagg which read, "You must win for me." Stagg told the players, and in the second half, Walter Eckersall punted over the goal. Michigan's Denny Clark fielded the ball, but Art Badenoch and Mark Catlin of Chicago tackled him in the end zone for a safety and the game's only points.

The following year, 1906, the forward pass was legalized, but Stagg already had 64 pass plays in his offense. He had begun shifting players – a tactic Knute Rockne later used to form the famed Notre Dame Shift and which Pop Warner made the basis of his single and double wing formations – and all of this helped him win 30 of 32 games from 1905 to 1909. Walter Steffen, one of Stagg's greatest players, along with Hugo Bezdek and Eckersall clinched the 1908 conference title by running 100 yards with a kickoff against Wisconsin.

Stagg won his final Big Ten title in 1924, and eight years later, at age 70, he was faced with mandatory retirement. The university's famed president, Robert K. Hutchins, offered Stagg an advisory post for $8000 a year. But Stagg wanted only to coach football, and such deals were anathema to his beliefs, so he moved to College of the Pacific (now University of the Pacific) in Stockton, Cali-

fornia as head coach for the next 14 years because he believed the school was free of commercialism. He riled many by scheduling the Pacific Coast's best teams, waiving off the criticism by noting, "You can't beat them if you don't schedule them." He returned to Chicago to play his old school in 1938, and his team won 32-0. In 1943, his team was ranked in the top ten, and at the age of 79, he was named Coach of the Year. He was carried off the field by his players after they upset Del Monte Pre-Flight, and chortled, "This hasn't happened since Yale beat Harvard in baseball in 1886!"

In 1946, he again was forced to retire because of age, and again turned down a stipend to act as an advisor, preferring instead, at age 88, to join his son, Amos Jr., as co-coach at Susquehanna College in Pennsylvania. Amos Jr. was a defensive specialist, and he turned the offense over to his dad, who thrived on ten-hour work days in this small college atmosphere where there were no perks, and few of the players had any experience. He drilled them as he had once drilled men who were now old enough to be their grandfathers, and supplied the inspirational qualities which has son lacked.

During this time, he returned to the West Coast each winter, and once met Fritz Crisler, Michigan's athletic director and a former player and assistant coach for him at Chicago, who kidded him about "being pretty old to sign any ten-year contracts."

"Fritz," he chuckled, "I'm looking forward to being able to renew it."

Left: *Stagg's son Amos Jr. (right) later hired his dad at age 88 to help him coach Susquehanna College. He had played quarterback for his dad at Chicago, along with Pat Page Jr. (left), son of assistant coach Pat Sr. (second from left).*

JOCK SUTHERLAND

Record:

Lafayette (1919-23)   33-8-2

Pittsburgh (1924-38)   111-20-12

He was called the "Old Man," "Silent Scot," "Great Stone Face," and "Sphinx of Football." Dr. John Bain (Jock) Sutherland also was called "great," an accolade he truly earned during a magnificent coaching career at Lafayette College and the University of Pittsburgh.

Jock Sutherland was by any standards a great American success story. As an 18-year-old youth, he came to the United States from his native Scotland at the behest of his older brother, who like so many elders, came to this country and worked hard enough to bring other family members here. The younger Sutherland worked at a variety of jobs for six years until he attended Oberlin Academy in Ohio for the preparatory education he needed to attend college, after which he heeded the advice of a Pitt football scout to enroll in that school. Sutherland knew nothing about football, and the first game he ever saw was the first one he ever played. A guard on Pop Warner's great Pitt teams, he was named All-America by Walter Camp as the Panthers went unbeaten in 1916.

Sutherland earned a degree as a dentist, and while he never so much as cleaned one tooth, while he coached at Lafayette from 1919 to 1923, he re-

Right: *Jock Sutherland led Pitt to its greatest success in football, taking the Panthers to five Rose Bowls en route to becoming the winningest coach in the school's history.*

turned every year to Pitt to teach at its School of Dentistry. In 1932, he was made a Fellow in the American College of Dentists, awarded for meritorious service and advancement in the science and art of dentistry.

After Sutherland was discharged from the Army in 1919, where he had his first taste of football coaching, he became head coach at Lafayette. His 1921 team won all nine games including a 6-0 victory over Warner's last great Pitt team that Jock ranked as his biggest coaching thrill. At Lafayette, he began to set the tone for his great teams at Pitt, teaching single wing football that he had learned from Warner, but without any of the deceptive frills. Warner later admitted that his former pupil "put more punch into his single wing play than any other coach."

Sutherland stressed tremendous precision and speed, and this became his hallmark in later years at Pitt when his teams featured a power attack. Pitt's deep reverse became one of football's great plays, because Sutherland literally machined and perfected a blocking wall to mow down potential tacklers. His off-tackle play was run with the same precision. "Our halfback took four steps parallel to the line, and cut into the hole on the fourth step on his outside foot," one Pitt player recalled. "Not the third or the fifth step, but the fourth."

Sutherland, at Lafayette and Pitt, was a perfectionist who believed in mastering a few plays. All of his plays were conservative, because he was a possession-type coach who did not believe in fancy re-

verses or laterals, and disdained the forward pass to such an extent that his Pitt team once played Ohio State and never threw the ball. His great 1921 team at Lafayette didn't throw a half-dozen passes during its 9-0 season. Sutherland also never ran a drill in practice that was not directly related to football. His players never ran wind sprints; instead, they ran signal drills in formations up and down the field.

Dubbed the "dour Scot" because of his very austere appearance that was compounded by his lean, hulking body and very pointed facial features, Sutherland intimidated most of his players with his strictness, aloof nature and a sharp tongue that trilled its r's with a fine Scottish burr. Most agreed that the cold, calculating way his team played football mirrored his public personality, as usually is the case with any great coach. His players especially knew him as a rigid disciplinarian who thrived on three things – hard work, perfection of detail, and spirit. He didn't take defeat lightly, and after his team was upset by Duquesne in 1936, he did not attend practice for three days, which further increased his players' anxiety, to the point that the team rebounded to defeat Notre Dame 20-0.

If a player argued with him to any length, or made a mistake in a fatal moment of any game, it was unpardonable. George Delich, a tackle on the great 1935-37 Pitt teams, erred in trying to tell Sutherland how to deploy his tackles against Notre Dame. He was benched for the final two games of his varsity career. Leo Malarkey, a nifty halfback,

fumbled on the goal line in the Duquesne upset, and he never started another game.

Yet, both players later became Sutherland's good friends, causing many to brand him an enigma. His close friends knew him as a man with some humor; he once told newsmen after miserable punting cost him the 1935 game against Notre

Far left: *Sutherland's greatest array of stars at Pitt was its Dream Backfield of (l-r) Harold Stebbins, John Chickerneo, Marshall Goldberg and Dick Cassiano. They led the Panthers to a Rose Bowl as sophs, were unbeaten as juniors and lost just once in their senior year.*

Left: *Sutherland, born and raised in Scotland, never saw a football game until he played in one and then won a scholarship to Pitt, where he earned a degree in dentistry.*

Above: *Marshall "Biggie" Goldberg was a Hall of Fame player for Sutherland at Pitt. A two-time All-American, he was a flashy runner with speed to the outside, and a terror when running trap plays to the inside.*

Dame: "When we punt, they don't have to move the ball. They just turn around the sticks, and it's first down going the other way." A lifelong bachelor, he considered Marshall "Biggie" Goldberg his greatest player and the son he never had; and others declared that he was a sensitive, sentimental guy who was hurt by the slightest criticism.

"I don't think he ever knew his players well," his great end, Bill Daddio, once noted. "He avoided that. He was very strict, he worked you hard, but he was very fair."

Following his tremendous success at Lafayette, Sutherland succeeded Pop Warner at Pitt. For the next 15 years, Sutherland, as one journalist noted, "became as much a part of Pittsburgh as the Golden Triangle . . . the bridges, the smoke, the coal mines, the steel mills . . . the Cathedral of Learning."

Four of his teams, usually playing against powerful opposition, were unbeaten, and after his first year, only four others lost more than two games in any season. After 1928, no Eastern team beat Pitt until Duquesne's 7-0 upset in 1936. In his fourth season, 1927, his team was unbeaten but lost to his old coach, Warner, 7-6 in the Rose Bowl, the first

of four appearances in Pasadena during his time at Pitt. Two years later, his team was unbeaten again but was smothered by Southern California, 47-14 in the Rose Bowl.

Sutherland's teams shone in the 1930s, and they thrived on great rivalries. He won five of six games from Notre Dame from 1932 through 1937, and in one game, Irish coach Elmer Layden got so steamed at watching Pitt's blockers mow down his safetyman on every play, that he rushed Sutherland, poked him in the chest and told him off. Jock was unmoved, and had the last silent word when Layden declared in very untypical Notre Dame fashion, "I'm through with Pitt. We haven't got a chance. They not only knock our ears back, but we are no good the following week." Who could blame him – the Irish were outscored 98-15, and were shut out in four of the six games.

Another national power at that time, Nebraska's Cornhuskers, was equally frustrated, never beating Pitt in 12 tries, with three of the games ending in ties. But none of the rivalries was more dynamic than Pitt's annual encounters with Fordham. Sutherland never lost, but the teams played three consecutive scoreless ties in 1935-37 when Fordham had its great Seven Blocks of Granite line. These games turned out record crowds in New York City and Pittsburgh. One of those ties, in 1937, was the only blemish on his team that season (Goldberg actually scored for Pitt that year, but the play was disallowed by a holding penalty). Pitt stunned the nation by rejecting a fifth Rose Bowl bid after having defeated Washington 21-0 the previous year. Sutherland and his players were still upset at the school's refusal to provide any spending money during that trip, and he dug into his own pocket to give each boy a few dollars.

Sutherland's crowning glory at Pitt was his famous Dream Backfield of Goldberg, Dick Cassiano, Harold (Curly) Stebbins and John Chickerneo. As sophomores, they led Pitt to a Rose Bowl victory; they went unbeaten in 1937; and just missed another perfect season in 1938 when, in the last game, Duke's unbeaten and unscored upon team defeated them 7-0 in a snowstorm in, of all places, Durham, North Carolina. This great backfield played behind an equally great line with such players as Tony Mattisi, Ave Daniell, Frank Souchak, Bill Glassford and Bill Daddio.

Sutherland, though, was having his own problems with Pitt's administration. The Rose Bowl expense situation still festered, and Pitt's administration, sensitive to criticism by some anti-football journalists, wanted a "strictly amateur" athletic policy, and to develop "a football team above criticism." He could not go along with this, and resigned in 1939, later becoming a very successful NFL coach until his death from a brain tumor in 1949.

JOHNNY VAUGHT

Record:

Mississippi (1947-70; 1973) 190-61-12

John Howard Vaught left an indelible mark on Southern football during his 24 seasons as head coach at the University of Mississippi. He was Number 2 nationally among active coaches with 185 victories when a heart attack forced him to step down from full-time coaching; his six Southeastern Conference titles were second in the league's history; he had raised Ole Miss football from Number 9 in the 12-team SEC standings to Number 3; his 1959 team was the SEC's Team of the Decade; and he developed 18 All-America players, and countless others who were accorded All-SEC recognition. He left a legacy of 14 consecutive bowl games, a national record, and 18 of his 24 teams participated in post-season games with a 10-8 record, setting two Sugar Bowl records in the process: most appearances (8) and most wins (5).

But all of that was just topping for a marvellous coaching career in which he was renowned for his offensive innovations and his ability to prepare a team thoroughly for any opponent. Certainly, the University of Tennessee, one of his fiercest rivals, still smarts when it recalls how its great 1970 team was ripped apart in a 38-0 Ole Miss victory when it was favored to win by a couple of TDs. Very simply, Vaught knew that the Vols would try to defense the outside play of quarterback Archie Manning, who loved to roll and throw, or run, so he built an attack that pulverized Tennessee's middle, hoping to force Tennessee to abandon its outside defenses and give Manning the edge he needed. All of that worked perfectly in a game that Vaught felt was as near-perfect as any of his teams ever played.

But this was as much a triumph for Vaught's uncanny ability to key a team psychologically as it was for his X's and O's. The year before, after Tennessee had beaten Mississippi 31-0, Steve Kiner, a Vols linebacker, bragged about how Manning's habit of tipping his receivers with his eyes made it easy for Tennessee's defense. For the next year, Archie worked to break the habit, but in the meantime, Kiner did Vaught's team another favor. He called them a "bunch of mules," and the wily old coach used that slur to goad his team to such a great effort. He even borrowed a mule and grazed it next to the team's practice field to serve as a constant reminder.

Vaught melded a wide array of philosophies that began with his own college coach at Texas Christian University, Francis Schmidt, who used the single and double wing, and spread formations, and then dozens of varieties of each; the absolute double wing devotion of Ray Wolf under whom he served at North Carolina Pre-Flight until Wolf was succeeded by Sleepy Jim Crowley, who imbued Vaught with the principles of the Notre Dame Box; the T formation from Larry (Moon) Mullins for whom he worked at Corpus Christi (Texas) Naval Air Station; and finally in 1946, while line coach at Alabama under Red Drew, the Tide's version of the Notre Dame Box, which had been espoused by Drew's predecessor, Frank Thomas, who had learned it from his coach and the system's originator, Knute Rockne.

When he inherited a great passer, Charley Conerly, in his first season at Mississippi, Vaught used his own version of the Notre Dame formation, forgoing his desire to put in the split-T until the following year. It was a great decision, because Conerly was not a great runner, but he and end Barney Poole set national passing records, finished 9-1, then defeated Texas Christian in the Delta Bowl.

Vaught was the first coach to use the split-T in the Deep South the following year, and as the 1950s evolved, he created the roll-out and sprint-out attacks, based primarily on a Wing-T forma-

Below: *Johnny Vaught melded several different offensive philosophies into a system that produced 190 victories at Mississippi. He developed 18 All-America players.*

tion. He even came up with something he dubbed the "E" and "L" formations. Always, Vaught utilized drop-back passing – he had fine quarterbacks such as Eagle Day, Jake Gibbs, Bobby Franklin and Manning for the job – but the moving pockets with the rollout style remained his favorite.

He always liked a wide open passing attack, part of his TCU heritage when he was an All-America guard back in the early 1930s, and flanked his wingbacks in 1947 so they made great targets for Conerly. Though the split-T was basically a full-house backfield attack, he soon sent halfbacks in motion to open the defenses; and the rollout and sprintout styles soon followed, along with flip-flopping receivers and backs in the late 1960s.

This made Ole Miss the South's great powerhouse from 1951 through 1963, when Vaught's teams won 111 games and lost only 19. They won a national title in 1960, five SEC titles, and began a run of 14 straight bowl appearances in 1957.

The team's rivalries with Louisiana State and Tennessee fascinated the nation. In 1958, LSU's national champions shut out Ole Miss 14-0 and a year later, on Halloween night with the Tigers still ranked Number 1, Heisman Trophy winner Billy Cannon returned a punt for the game's only touchdown, and LSU's defense stopped Mississippi at the goal line in a 7-3 victory. But Vaught got even in a Sugar Bowl rematch with a dominating 21-0 victory in which LSU showed a minus 15 yards rushing and was never in the game.

The Rebs were ranked second in 1959, and were acclaimed national champions the following year by the Football Writers Association of America following a 9-0-1 record (the tie was 6-6 against LSU on two field goals by center Allen Green, the second with six seconds to play), and a 14-6 win against Rice in the Sugar Bowl. Two years later, Vaught had the first perfect season ever for a Mississippi team, that included a 17-13 win over Arkansas in the Sugar Bowl.

This may have been Vaught's best coaching job,

Right: *Archie Manning was the last in a long line of fine passers developed by Vaught. Others were Charley Conerly, Jake Gibbs, Eagle Day and Bobby Franklin.*

because not only was his team filled with sopho-mores, but the distractions on the campus were rampant with federal forces present for most of that fall as the government enforced its anti-segre-gation policies. Hundreds of mediamen scurried about day-after-day causing further distraction, and federal forces actually "stood guard" over the team's practices as helicopters daily churned over-head in a sometimes deafening cacophony of sound that made teaching and concentrating nearly im-possible at times. Furthermore, no home games were permitted until November 10.

Vaught, of course, had his own favorite moments, and topping the list was his team's 21-14 victory over top-ranked Maryland in 1952, ending a 22-game Ter-rapin winning streak. "We really made a big step upward in prestige and recognition, and that win gave us a boost in many ways," he said.

"The year before, we beat Kentucky 21-17 at Oxford and we were a big underdog, and that got us going on that great streak of winning seasons. Our 39-7 victory over Texas in the 1958 Sugar Bowl was our first win in that game after losses to Geor-gia Tech and Navy a few years earlier, and our 14-13 victory over TCU in the 1956 Cotton Bowl was our first major bowl victory."

Vaught had always driven himself to be a winner,

starting as a youth in Fort Worth, Texas when his grandmother took him into her home, told him to quit his job as a red cap at the Santa Fe depot and go to school. Soon thereafter, he played his first foot-ball game and lost 40-0 to a team from a local orphanage. His uncle, Edell Harris, chided Vaught about losing to a bunch of "little bitty orphans," but even in his youthful misery, he realized that those kids ate, slept and lived as a family unit. Years later when he became head coach at Mississippi, he built his football team as a family. He once raised some eyebrows when he said that if a boy came to Ole Miss to play football and left the school, there was something wrong with the boy. He never backed down from that stance.

Yet, he was known for "turning the other cheek" by always giving a player the benefit of the doubt and furnishing him with either a second or third chance. He considered other things important for the athlete's good in that he always insisted that his players get their degrees, regardless of the extra expense to his department.

However, he was intolerant of poor perform-ance and asked only that a player do his best. He also asked that a player always conduct himself as a gentleman. These were his two favorite recruiting statements, and they were enough.

Above: *All-America end Barney Poole (18) played for a season at Mississippi before enjoying a great career at West Point. He returned to Mississippi under Vaught, continued his All-America play and became a Hall of Famer.*

WALLACE WADE

Record:

Alabama (1923-30)	61-13-3
Duke (1931-41)	85-19-3
(1946-50)	25-17-4

In 1923, college football in the East, most of the Midwest, and on the West Coast was highly respected. No one really cared too much about football in the South, and particularly at the University of Alabama. While that sounds a bit incongruous nearly seven decades later, considering that football is king in Dixie, and that Alabama need not take a back seat to any school for fame and recognition, that rise to prominence had its roots in just one man: William Wallace Wade.

Wade came to Alabama after two years as an assistant coach to Dan McGugin at Vanderbilt, and began a coaching reign that netted the Crimson Tide three unbeaten seasons, three national championships, three Rose Bowl titles and seven Southern Conference crowns when that conference

embraced every major college in the South (it later split off into the Southeastern Conference, and later the remaining Southern Conference split to form the Atlantic Coast Conference). Then he brought Duke its greatest years with six more Southern Conference titles, two unbeaten regular seasons, and a couple of Rose Bowl victories. Long before he finished his coaching career at Duke in 1950, the success that Wade produced marked the South as the hotbed of college football.

Wade perfectly fits the mold as one of the game's greatest coaches, because he was an exacting teacher and a single-minded leader who didn't peek right or left in keeping his sights set on winning. He shunned coaching histrionics, stressing efficiency; and he was deaf to excuses, preferring to talk about production. He summarily dismissed the losing-builds-character group. "What good did it ever do anyone to get kicked around?" he asked.

Of course, he never got kicked around too much. In his 23 years as a head coach, he lost only two games that could be considered blowouts, 25-0 to Syracuse by his first Alabama team and 25-2 to Tennessee by his first Duke team. Of his 36 losses at Duke, 22 were by one touchdown or less.

He was a drillmaster at practice, sometimes running the same play ten consecutive times if he believed his players had not mastered it. If doubts lingered, the play was dumped from the week's game plan and might not appear for a month. He perfected the timing of every play with a metro-

Below: *Wallace Wade sent Alabama on its way to national prominence during eight seasons by winning 61 games, three national championships and three Rose Bowls.*

Above: *Wade was a member of Brown University's 1916 team that played in what most consider the first Rose Bowl game. The Bruins are shown arriving in Chicago en route home from losing to Washington State.*

nome, and often got down on the ground with a player to show him precisely how his blocking technique must work. It was little wonder that he was considered an expert on the fundamentals of blocking and tackling.

Like all great coaches, he had a flexibility that allowed him to react to changing situations. In 1935, he was at odds with Carl Snavely, the head coach at arch-rival North Carolina, and desperately wanted to knock the Tar Heels out of Rose Bowl contention. He completely switched tactics and, contrary to his personality, actually joked about an opponent, for the only time in his career. His team was so flabbergasted with this approach that it went out loose and easy, and stunned UNC 25-0. Against Wake Forest in 1936, he alternated the first and second team during the first half, and the varsity did little. At halftime, he told his second team, "Gentlemen, I'm afraid to start the first team, so I'm going to leave the room and let you decide which team should start the second half." Naturally, the second team voted to start, and Wade kept them in until his regulars had reached the height of apoplexy before sending them in. Duke won 20-0. When he lost all-America tailback George McAfee before the 1938 season, he immediately dropped the focus of his planning from offense. "We depended on punting, punt returns, blocking punts and defense," Wade said later. The result: Duke shut out every opponent!

Though he insisted on perfection, he often lamented an over-emphasis on winning. He believed football was only a part of a man-building program at the college level, and at Duke, he started an elaborate physical education program which gave every student a chance to study and participate in his favorite sports.

All of this was consistent in the way he conducted his life. He was born in Trenton, Tennessee, and finished his high school education at Chicago's Morgan Park Academy before enrolling at Brown University. He worked his way through college, counting every nickel as he went, and it is said that he walked several miles to football practice each day to save trolley fare. Though undersized, he became a starting guard on Brown's great 1916 team that played in the Rose Bowl, and lost to Washington State. He later avenged that slight when his 1930 Alabama team defeated the Cougars in the Rose Bowl and claimed its third national championship.

World War I was being fought, and Wade enlisted in the Army after graduation and became a captain at age 25, though he never saw any combat because the war ended while he was still training with the cavalry. His brief military experience touched him, though, because he left coaching in 1942 during World War II, and organized and trained the 272nd Field Artillery Battalion. When the war ended, Lt. Col. Wallace Wade's battalion had fought with the First, Third and Ninth Armies in the Battle of Normandy, the Siegfried Line, the Battle of the Bulge, at the crossing of the Rhine, and was at the Elbe River, just 60 miles from Berlin when the war ended. He received the U.S. Bronze Star and the Croix de Guerre with Palm from France.

The fact that he could endure the rigors of fighting in a world war in his fifties was just another example of Wade's determination to succeed. It was no different when, after two years on McGugin's staff at Vanderbilt, he was sought by both Alabama and Kentucky for the head coaching job. He went through the interview session with the athletic board at Lexington, Kentucky, and then was asked to wait in an anteroom while the members considered his qualifications. When, after an hour, no decision had been reached, Wade's patience had expired and he pounded on the door of the meeting room – just as the commitee had dropped its secret ballots into a hat from which they would be counted. "I'm tired of waiting, because either you want me or you don't," he told the startled board members. "I'm going to Alabama, and Kentucky will never win a game from me."

He beat the Wildcats eight times at Alabama, and three more times at Duke before Kentucky simply stopped scheduling his team. Ironically, after he had stormed out of the meeting at Kentucky, the board members decided to count the ballots anyway, and he had been a unanimous choice!

He finished second in the Southern Conference during his first year at Alabama, whose only previous claim to national glory was a 9-7 upset of Penn the previous season. He won the conference the next two years, and his 1926 team surrendered only one touchdown in winning nine games before it was invited to play Washington in the Rose Bowl.

Johnny Mack Brown, later a great movie cowboy star, was a great outside runner for Alabama. But when the Tide trailed 19-0 at the half, Wade shifted the emphasis of attack from him to Pooley Hubert pounding the middle, and mixed in some passes. He put two guards at end to stop the Huskies' punishing off-tackle play, and got three touchdowns in seven minutes of the third quarter en route to a 20-19 victory and the national title.

Alabama went unbeaten the following season, and again was invited to the Rose Bowl where a 7-7 tie against Pop Warner's great Stanford team got it a second national title. This sudden surge to glory quickly spoiled the Tide's fans, and there was plenty of grumbling when Wade's teams were 17-10-1 in the next three seasons. That was enough for

him, and he decided to move to Duke after the 1930 season, vowing to go out in a blaze of glory. He did, with a 9-0 record, a 13-6 victory in the Rose Bowl over Washington State, and a national title.

Before Wade arrived in 1931, Duke, known as Trinity College until 1925, had had only four winning seasons after starting a full-fledged schedule in 1921; Wade had only one losing season, in 1946, in 16 years. The 1936 team, which lost only to Tennessee and shut out seven opponents in winning nine games, was his first great one, featuring All-America tailback Clarence (Ace) Parker, Elmore Hackney and Eric Tipton.

The 1938 team hadn't allowed a point as it came to the final game of the season against Jock Sutherland's great Pitt team that featured its Dream Backfield of Marshall Goldberg, Curly Stebbins, John Chickerneo, Dick Cassiano and Frank Patrick. Wade concentrated his defensive plans solely on stopping the Panthers' running game, and he ordered Tipton to kick to all four corners of the field every day for three weeks before the game. Wade's sliding defense shut down Pitt's runners, and Tipton punted the ball out of bounds seven times inside Pitt's 10-yard line. Duke won 7-0 when

Left: *Wade (left) had only one losing season in 16 years at Duke. A severe taskmaster on the practice field, his work paid off when his 1937 team did not allow a point until the final minute of the Rose Bowl game.*

Left: *George McAfee was one of the stars of Duke's great teams in 1938 and 1939 that lost just two games in two seasons. He later was a great running back for the Chicago Bears of the NFL.*

end Bolo Perdue blocked Goldberg's punt for a TD.

Duke took its perfect record to the Rose Bowl against Southern California, and it lasted until, with 40 seconds to play, Doyle Nave passed to Al Krueger for a 7-0 USC victory.

Wade got one more Rose Bowl trip, on January 1, 1942, only his team travelled no further than from its dorms to Duke's stadium. Pearl Harbor had been attacked only three weeks before, and the West Coast feared a Japanese attack, so all events attracting crowds were banned. Wade, having already been invited to play Oregon State after a 9-0 season, convinced the committee to shift the game to Durham. Duke lost 20-16 in a thrilling game.

Wade returned to Duke as athletic director after the war ended in Europe in 1945 while Eddie Cameron finished his last season as interim coach. He took over in 1946, but he had changed his perspective on the game. "He found it increasingly difficult to ask 200-pound athletes to give their all for Duke when he had seen 150-pound GIs dying for their country," one friend noted. Wade retired after the 1950 season to become commissioner of the Southern Conference, and in 1967, he saw the stadium at Duke, where he had so many great moments, renamed in his honor. He was later inducted into the Hall of Fame, and died in 1986 at the age of 94.

LYNN (PAPPY) WALDORF

Record:

Oklahoma City University (1925-27)	17-11-3
Oklahoma State (1929-33)	34-10-7
Kansas State (1934)	7-2-1
Northwestern (1935-46)	49-45-7
California (1947-56)	67-32-4

"You can be the greatest coach in America and simply be at the wrong school. And a good coach in the wrong situation gets fired," Michigan coach Bo Schembechler warned some of his peers a few years ago, while they sat around exchanging thoughts on their often precarious and fragile profession. The words hit home, and some present began casting about for the names of coaches who made a habit of rising far above the jobs they held.

Suddenly, someone blurted out two words: "Pappy Waldorf!" and then added, "Considering what he did and where he was, Pappy Waldorf may have been the greatest football coach of all time."

Every school at which he coached had a reputation for being a "coaching graveyard," yet Lynn (Pappy) Waldorf's winning percentage was far above the average at each school. He also won championships in every conference in which he

coached. Waldorf began his career at Oklahoma City University, which had gone 1-23-1 in three previous seasons. By 1927, Waldorf's team won a share of the conference title. Waldorf next coached at Oklahoma State, which hadn't had a winning season in five years (and didn't have one for five more years after he left), and he won or shared four Missouri Valley championships. At Kansas State for a year, Waldorf's Wildcats won the school's only conference title ever. Northwestern had three straight losing seasons and had won only three games the season before Waldorf arrived in 1935. He was named Coach of the Year in his first season, and in his second, he won the school's last Big Ten title and remains Northwestern's winningest coach. California had had eight straight losing seasons before Waldorf showed up in 1947, and his first four teams had a 38-4-1 record, made three trips to the Rose Bowl and won two Pacific Coast Conference championships.

The son of a Methodist bishop, Waldorf had given thoughts to a business career before coaching intruded after he had twice won All-America honors playing tackle for Syracuse University in the mid-1920s. But football was as much a part of the Waldorf family as the Bible, because four of his brothers played football, and three of them also became head coaches.

Waldorf was a bespectacled man of large girth, with an ever-present cigar, but with an outlook that more suited a clergyman than someone working in the often wacky world of football. His perspective was that football is a game and should be treated like one, and he wanted the players to enjoy it. He made sure that not a day went by that the players and coaches didn't have something to laugh about during the practice sessions, if only to relieve some of the drudgery and renew sagging spirits. Away from the field, he also believed that football was just one facet of college life for those who played it, and that their prime responsibility was to succeed in the classroom, and then partake in a variety of outlets available to all students.

Waldorf was renowned for maintaining a calm and sane demeanor around his players, regardless of how badly things may have gone the previous week. He was a patient teacher who must have set some kind of record when, it is said, he didn't bawl out a single player during his first two seasons at Northwestern. In fact, he probably salvaged himself a fine quarterback when he didn't banish Fred Vanzo in 1935 after he had fumbled and lost the ball on the one-yard line, helping Purdue to a 7-0 victory. Vanzo blamed himself and was not much good after that turnover, but Waldorf "nursed" him back to the proper outlook a quarterback needs on the field, and he went on to be an All-Big Ten selection in 1936, having helped lead the Wildcats to the Big Ten championship.

Below: *Lynn (Pappy) Waldorf started as an All-America tackle at Syracuse, and went on to win five different conference titles at the five schools at which he coached.*

Left: *Waldorf and his 1945 Northwestern team. Pappy won Coach of the Year honors in his first season with the Wildcats, impressing electors with his work despite a so-so 4-3-1 record.*

Below: *Waldorf stunned the Big Ten in 1936 as his Wildcats went unbeaten till the final game of the season, which they lost to Notre Dame. Here, Larry Danbom of the Irish is tackled by Don Heap (22) of Northwestern.*

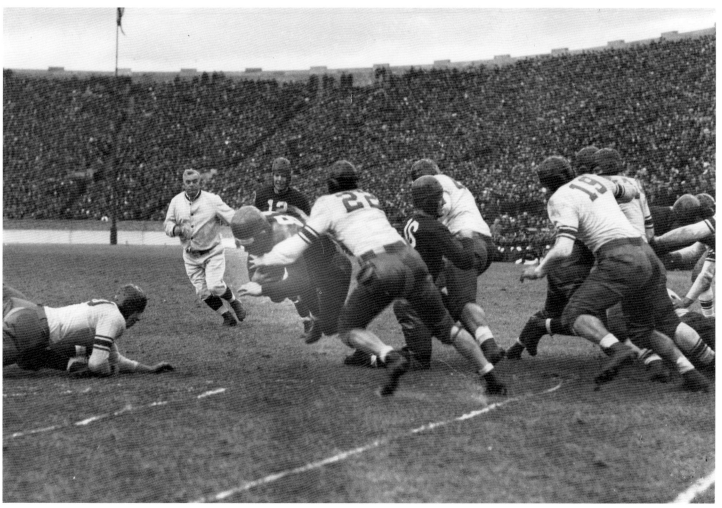

Above: *Waldorf took over a Northwestern team that hadn't had a winning season in three years, and turned in a 4-3-1 record. Some of his players included, from left: Steve Toth, Don Geyer, Paul Tangora, Al Lind, Wally Cruice and Bill Bogger.*

This is not to say that Waldorf was a pushover, because he was firm on one thing: Consistency. He would be patient and try to help a player with his calm teaching methods as long as the boy made progress, believing he would be more effective by winning the player's confidence than by being a martinet. But if the player showed a proclivity to repeat errors, then Waldorf could cut him off without blinking an eye.

He was also renowned for his organization. He would lay out in almost minute detail precisely what the team would work on each day. Most believe this was the underlying key to his ability to quickly turn around losing programs, because he focused precisely on the areas which needed constant attention. One other factor was his "bread-and-butter" approach to the game. He didn't go for frills or fancy plays, believing the best play was one that went straight ahead, and the worst play was the one that didn't.

While he was very successful at his first three coaching stops, it was at Northwestern before World War II, and at the University of California in Berkeley after the war, that Waldorf gained his greatest fame. His impact at Northwestern was immediate – the Wildcats defeated previously unbeaten Notre Dame 14-7, their first victory over the Irish in 35 years. The Coach of the Year electors were so impressed with the job he did in carving out a modest 4-3-1 record that they bypassed Bernie Bierman, who won the national championship at Minnesota, and Princeton's Fritz Crisler, who had his second undefeated team in three seasons.

In 1936, led by Don Heap and Don Geyer – the "Dashing Dons" – Waldorf's teams blitzed the Big Ten beginning with back-to-back wins over Ohio State and Illinois, before ending Minnesota's 30-game unbeaten streak, 6-0, the only TD the Gophers allowed that season in Big Ten competition. Only a season-ending loss to Notre Dame cost them a perfect season.

Waldorf stunned everyone when he left Northwestern in 1947 for California, acknowledging that he was leaving a "sure job" but still unable to bypass "a challenge unequalled anywhere." He had that "challenge" under control immediately, winning nine of ten games in 1947, and then sent Cal on a three-season unbeaten streak that reached 38 games in regular season competition. He was helped immediately by two of college football's great players back in the 1940s, fullback Jackie Jensen and guard Rod Franz. Jensen, who went on to an outstanding major league baseball career, averaged more than seven yards per carry in leading his team to a perfect season in 1948. Waldorf always declared that this team was evenly balanced, but certain players rose to the fore in key situations. When Cal beat Washington on a muddy field, Jack Swaner scored three touchdowns; and two weeks later, in beating Southern Cal, 13-7, quarterback Dick Erickson engineered a 12-play, 88-yard drive that Waldorf called "the best single drive against a tough opponent I witnessed during my years at Cal."

Waldorf lost to his old Northwestern team in the Rose Bowl in a game of big plays – a record 73-yard TD run by the Wildcats' Frank Aschenbrenner, one of 67 yards by Jensen, and finally, with three minutes to play, the game-winner of 43 yards by Ed Tunnicliff.

Waldorf lost Jensen to major league baseball in 1949, but turned in his second straight unbeaten season, patching and filling as injuries cut down his offensive stars. Charlie Sarver, who averaged ten yards a carry in his first four games, went down with a knee injury. Jack Swaner was lost for all but one game, but in that one, against Stanford, he scored three touchdowns in a come-from-behind victory. Frank Brunk returned a kickoff 102 yards

against Southern Cal after the Trojans had just gone ahead 10-7 in the last quarter. The Bears shared the PCC title with Oregon State, but they got the nod to the Rose Bowl, and again were nosed out in the last minute, 17-14, by Ohio State, when the Buckeyes forced a bad punt deep in Cal's territory and turned the opportunity into the winning field goal.

Waldorf had a 9-0-1 season in 1950 (he was 38-1-1 in regular season play during his first four seasons) and lost his third Rose Bowl game, 14-6 to Michigan. But he had proven that good coaches sometimes can survive, and excel, in football graveyards.

Above: *One of Waldorf's stars at Northwestern was running back Bill DeCorrevont.*

Below: *Jackie Jensen (with ball), an All-America fullback for the 1948 California team, was Waldorf's greatest player.*

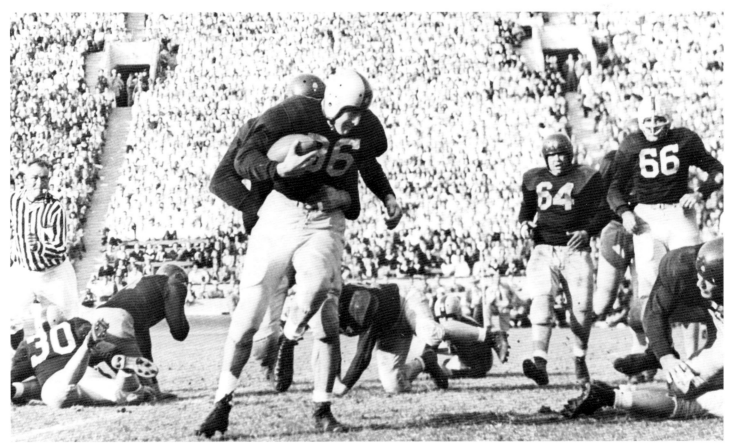

GLENN S. (POP) WARNER

Record:

Georgia (1895-96)	7-4-0
Cornell (1897-98)	15-5-1
(1904-06)	21-8-2
Carlisle (1899-1903)	34-18-3
(1907-14)	74-23-5
Pitt (1915-23)	59-11-44
Stanford (1924-32)	71-17-8
Temple (1933-38)	31-18-9

At age 25, he was nicknamed "Pop." Four decades later, Glenn Scobey Warner was considered one of the fathers of American football.

Warner was the single biggest tactical influence on the game during the first 40 years of this century with his invention of both the single and double wing formations, the remnants of which are still seen today in the so-called "shotgun" formations which many college and professional teams use in passing situations. A few colleges still employ his single wing formation – and with great success, since opponents must find a way to create and master a new defense for just one game.

Warner, along with Amos Alonzo Stagg, Dr. Harry Williams and Bob Zuppke, were part of a rare inventive breed who guided the growth of football from its rugby and soccer backgrounds and introduced offensive concepts which made the game much more interesting for spectators. In addition, he was among an elite group of early coaches who developed ways and means of improving the game, such as use of a huddle, "dummy scrimmage," spiralling a punt and forward pass for great distance, the use of helmets, and the body block.

Best of all, he is forever linked with one of America's greatest athletes, Jim Thorpe, whom he coached at the Carlisle Indian School in Pennsylva-

Right: *Glenn Scobey (Pop) Warner is the fourth winningest coach in college football history, and one of its greatest innovators with his invention of the single and double wing formations.*

nia. In fact, Warner is probably best remembered for his work at Carlisle, a tiny Pennsylvania college which competed on equal terms with the biggest schools in the East and Midwest during the 13 years that he coached there.

Almost forgotten are his great teams at Pitt, some claim greater even than those of Jock Sutherland's powerhouses of the 1930s, and his success at Stanford, where his second most famous player, Ernie Nevers, was a great star during the 1920s. Nearly lost also is the fact that Warner ranks Number 4 on the list of all-time winningest coaches, and was Number 2 until Bear Bryant, and then Eddie Robinson, moved into the top two spots in the 1980s. His 43-year coaching career produced 312 victories, just two behind Stagg.

Stagg, Zuppke, Williams, Knute Rockne and Fielding Yost were his contemporaries for all or part of the first three decades of his career, and with the exception of the magnetic Rockne, Warner was the most publicized coach in college football during most of his career. During the golden age of sports in the 1920s, Warner and Rockne were the two magic names of coaching, each the author of a system of football that gathered legions of disciples.

Rockne, of course, had the famed "Notre Dame Box," or "Shift Formation," while Warner offered a pair of wingback formations which he laced with a series of reverses, balanced and unbalanced lines, and great power at any point of attack along a defense's front line.

Their two systems were as different as the men themselves. Rockne's "shift" formation was based on speed and getting off with everyone moving at the snap of the ball, while Warner moved people around and dared a defense to match the movement, or cope with straight-ahead power and blocking. Warner was not the magnetic, vibrant personality that made Rockne a national treasure, and he lacked the inspirational fervor and the mastery of psychology that turned Rockne from coach to legend. He also was not a dominant, forceful leader of men, though he engendered deep-seated loyalty and affection from his players that few could match.

Warner was far more contemplative and deliberate in his thinking than Rockne, who had a great flair for the quick phrase and a penetrating wit which perfectly suited the age in which he coached. Warner's style reflected his off-field hobby of rebuilding worn-out automobile engines: in the quiet of his study, he tinkered with the X's and O's that filled his notepads, and then made those symbols come alive on the field with players expertly placed for solid offensive performance. Everything that came off those notepads was innovative and unorthodox in the context of the game as it was played at that time, because he created a wide-

open offense where speed, deception and quick-thinking became necessities.

Nowhere was this more telling than at Carlisle, where he coached fast and comparatively light Native American athletes. It was here that Warner

Left: Warner's greatest early player was Jim Thorpe at the Carlisle Indian School. Thorpe played five seasons for Warner against the best competition in America.

Overleaf: Warner (second row, third from left) played for Cornell in 1893 and returned four years later as head coach, winning 15 games in two seasons. His greatest years as coach and innovator came after he left Cornell for Carlisle, Pitt and Stanford.

first worked out his single wing formation, in which one side of the offensive line was overbalanced with two tackles placed between a guard and end, while the other side of the line had just a guard and end outside the center. He placed a back behind the end on the strong side of the line to help him block or come back toward the middle to take part in inside plays, handoffs for reverses or to lead blocking. A second back, the blocking back or quarterback, lined up behind the guard on the strong side; the fullback was placed five yards behind him, and a tailback six yards behind the center.

Warner didn't stop there, because he took the deep halfback, or tailback, and placed him behind the end on the weak side, leaving just the fullback lined up behind center. This became his double wing formation, which was good for reverses from either side, fakes, fullback spinner plays, and straight ahead running by a strong fullback.

The double wing formation, which Warner used at Carlisle and Pitt, didn't get notoriety until he moved to Stanford in the mid-1920s, and played Notre Dame in the 1925 Rose Bowl. Warner used it exclusively that day, and although his team lost, Nevers was a great offensive threat, and an entire nation became aware of the play's potential as Ernie outrushed the fabled Four Horsemen with 114 yards and Stanford had 17 first downs to just six for Rockne's team.

Warner brought two more teams to the Rose Bowl, tying Alabama 7-7 in 1927 and defeating Pitt

7-6 the following year. Then he brought his team to New York City, the first time a West Coast team had ever played there, where it met Army at Yankee Stadium. The Cadets had the fabulous Red Cagle at halfback, but he was no match for Warner's variety of passes, spinners, double and triple reverses as Stanford blitzed the once-beaten Cadets 26-0. The next year, the Warner system reached epidemic proportions on the coaching blackboards across the nation.

When he coached at Carlisle, Warner found he had some willing students who found football a perfect game in which to try and outwit the "palefaces" at other schools, and in their own minds, at least, gain some measure of vindication for what had happened to their forefathers during the previous three centuries.

"I unveiled the single wing concept against Army in 1912," Warner once said, "and if there was one team the Indians liked to beat more than any other, it was Army. That day, our concepts were brilliantly successful and we won 27-6, mainly because our wingback was so adept at blocking Army's tackle and giving us plenty of room with our sweeps. Army never fathomed what we tried to do."

Jim Thorpe started at Carlisle as a substitute in 1907, and was a regular the following year. Warner said Thorpe, at 178 pounds, "had speed as well as strength, and knew how to use them as well as any athlete I ever knew. He was a great runner, but

Below: Warner ran a tight program at Stanford and often barred visitors and press from his practices.

Below right: Stanford All-America running back Ernie Nevers was Warner's greatest all-around player because, unlike Jim Thorpe, he played all-out in every game.

also a great kicker as his four field goals in a 17-0 victory over mighty Harvard in 1908 indicated. He had everything. He was a star punter, a star drop-kicker, a star passer. No one ever excelled more in blocking or running around end."

Warner's only gripe with Thorpe was his laziness at times, for which reason he accorded Nevers the honor of being the greatest player he ever coached. In modern terms, Thorpe was a 10-second, 100-yard dash man, durable to the point of never missing any time because of injury. He was the perfect athlete to make Warner's system successful.

After his second tour at Carlisle, Warner went to Pitt and made the Panthers a colossus in Eastern football, winning his first 29 games before losing to the Cleveland Naval Reserves 9-6 in the final game of the 1918 season. Pitt was penalized on nearly every play, and in the fourth quarter, miscalls by the officials prolonged play for some 44 minutes, enabling the Navy team to win. Warner called his 1916 team the "best of all time," with such stars as Tiny Thornhill, Jock Sutherland, Bob Peck, Pud Seidel, George McLaren and Jimmy DeHart. In 1918, that team ended a four-year unbeaten streak by Georgia Tech, 32-0. A year later, the Panthers were beaten by Penn State 20-0, but not before Warner nailed Nittany Lions coach Hugo Bezdek's habit of placing his bench right on the sidelines so

he could counsel his players when they came for water. Coaching players on the field was against the rules at the time, so Warner foiled Bezdek by nailing Penn State's benches to six-foot posts back by the stands at Pitt Stadium. It didn't get him a victory, but he at least got the best of one of his bitter rivals.

While coaching at Pitt, Warner was offered a great deal at Stanford, which he accepted. But not wishing to leave the Panthers in the midst of a contract, he dispatched his assistant, Andy Kerr, to Palo Alto to coach his new team for two years, until he arrived to take over. Kerr won 11 of 18 games, and his team used the exact system that Warner preached, so that when he arrived in 1924, Stanford never skipped a beat, and ruled the West Coast for the next six seasons.

Warner finished his career at Temple, leading the Owls to their only bowl game after a 7-3 season in 1935. He was 68 years old when he finally retired from coaching in 1938, but his career, in addition to his 312 victories, was replete with innovations that served the game through its maturing years and stamped him as one of its greatest coaches. Perhaps his greatest legacy is the fact that hundreds of youth teams play in a national Pop Warner League organization, training future stars in a mode that Warner himself would have loved as a gruff, clever old coach who everyone called "Pop."

Above: *Warner's last six seasons as head coach were at Temple University, where he took the Owls to their first post-season play in the first Sugar Bowl game, against Tulane.*

BUD WILKINSON

Record:

Oklahoma (1947-63) 139-27-4

From 1948 through 1958, college football's most dominant team was the Oklahoma Sooners, a team which had winning streaks of 31 and 47 games; four perfect seasons; was unbeaten every year in conference play; won six of seven post-season games; scored 300 or more points in eight of those seasons; and whirled through opponents with a split-T formation offense that was as dazzling to watch as it was nearly impossible to contain.

In stark contrast, Charles (Bud) Wilkinson, the coach who ran this football blitzkrieg, was quiet and reserved. He had to be talked into returning to coaching after World War II by Oklahoma head coach Jim Tatum, whom he had known in the Navy. One year later, Tatum left for Maryland to succeed Bear Bryant, and Wilkinson was named head coach of the Sooners. But despite his tremendous success, he never really felt comfortable with the vagaries of his profession, and while still in the prime of his career, left after the 1963 season for an ill-fated venture into politics, and later was a highly respected network football commentator.

The way in which Wilkinson coached his teams was overshadowed by the tremendous results they produced. He disdained records and winning streaks, once noting: "The thing I'm proudest of is the type of boy represented at Oklahoma in football . . . A boy of character, a boy who first must be a

Right: *Bud Wilkinson and his Oklahoma teams were the greatest offensive producers in college football during the late 1940s and 1950s. No team used the split T with more efficiency.*

good enough student to do college work without undue difficulty, and to be able to graduate from college.

"There are a tremendous number of young men who are blessed with an abundance of physical energy and a truly combative spirit. They have to relieve themselves of that pressure and test their minds and bodies. Football fulfills that demand for total effort, and teaches them fair play, discipline, teamwork and loyalty."

With this insight, Wilkinson built his great teams, always stressing teamwork over individual glory. "There aren't enough heroic positions on a football team to have people play because they want to be a hero," he said. "The majority play because they love the game."

Wilkinson turned this "love of the game" into one powerhouse after another. He fashioned his offense from what he had learned playing for three years, the first two as a guard and the third as a blocking back, on Bernie Bierman's national champion single wing teams at Minnesota in the mid-1930s; and then added the principles of the split-T from Don Faurot, its inventor, with whom

Above: *Wilkinson (center) and his coaching staff at Oklahoma. From left, Frank (Pop) Ivy, George Lynn, Gomer Jones and Bill Jennings. Jones succeeded his boss as head coach in 1964.*

Left: *Wilkinson had been an All-America blocking back and guard on Bernie Bierman's national championship teams at Minnesota during the 1930s. The Split-T system he developed at Oklahoma was in direct contrast to Bierman's power-oriented single wing.*

Right: Wilkinson (left) was selected as Coach of the Year in 1949 after his team's perfect season, that also included a 35-0 victory over LSU in the Sugar Bowl. It was the first of his four perfect seasons at Oklahoma.

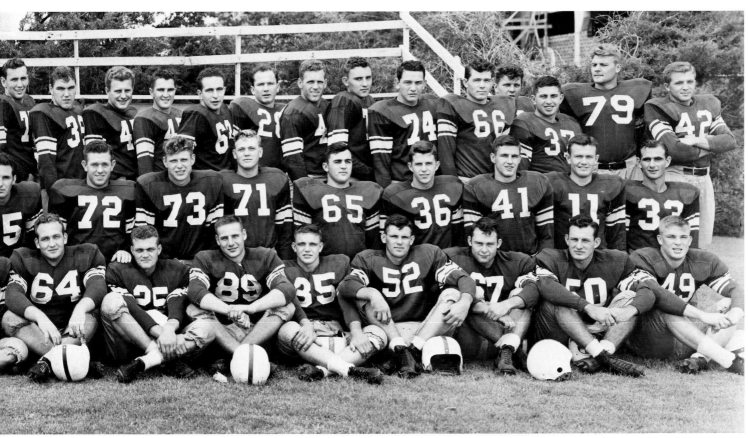

Above: *Oklahoma's 1949 team won 11 games and produced five All-Americans, including Darrell Royal (second row, second from right).*

Right: *Running back Billy Vessels won the Heisman Trophy in 1952 and was the key to Wilkinson's 8-1-1 season. Vessels scored 35 TDs that year.*

he worked as an assistant coach at Iowa Pre-Flight in 1943, prior to serving on the aircraft carrier USS *Enterprise* during some of the most vicious naval battles in World War II.

"I learned 99 percent of my football from Bierman, not only from the morale point but technically," said Wilkinson, who also coached under Ossie Solem at Syracuse, Dr. George Hauser at Minnesota, Faurot and his predecessor at Oklahoma, Jim Tatum. "He always said, 'Base your play on the standards most likely to defeat the champions. The good ones don't take the fake. You've got to block 'em.'"

This philosophical combination revolutionized offensive football in colleges during the late 1940s and 1950s because for the first time, the offense adjusted the play and the point of attack after the ball was snapped. In the past, the offense always tried to set up a defense with a series of moves to get it to react to an opposite move. In Wilkinson's system, the defense made its commitment, then the Sooners' ball carrier reacted away from it anywhere from between the guards to outside the defensive tackle.

Above: *Wilkinson learned the principles of the Split-T from Don Faurot, its originator, when the two served together in the Navy during World War II, but still credited Bernie Bierman, his old college coach, with teaching him the most about coaching success.*

"I also liked it because it was taught more effectively than any other offense in the short period of practice time we had, and because its fluid pattern of play enabled the individual linemen to move at will laterally," he said.

Wilkinson's system had one other great ingredient – blazing speed at nearly every position, but always in the backfield, so that when a back found the opening in the defense, there was little time to recover and hold him to a short gain. His teams also operated at a faster pace than their opponents. After returning the opening kickoff against Army in 1961, the Sooners sprinted out of their huddle and ran the first play for a touchdown while some of the Cadets were still moving to their positions. It was the difference in a 14-8 victory.

Wilkinson insisted that his players always be in peak condition. For one thing, his team played in the Oklahoma heat for at least half of the season; and for another, the pace of their game demanded tremendous stamina. Wilkinson also wanted players who could make big plays late in a game, and always pointed to an amazing blocking effort by fullback Buck McPhail against Nebraska in 1952.

McPhail led halfback Billy Vessels around right end, and wiped out the defender. But Vessels, hemmed in, cut back the other way and McPhail then blocked a defensive back to give him more room. As Vessels zoomed around left end, he was closely pursued by a Husker defender, so McPhail cut across the field and threw his third block on the same play, allowing Vessels to score. "When a player keeps looking for something to do after two blocks," Wilkinson said, "you know he's in good shape and has desire."

A Wilkinson paradox was his stress on defense over offense. His teams often led the nation in rushing offense as well as rushing defense, and 46 of his 139 victories were shutouts. Three of his teams posted five shutouts in one season, and his great 1956 team had six. This reflected his strongly-held belief that "it takes a man to play defense. Anybody can play offense, but we never talked to our kids about it until we taught them everything we knew about defense."

Wilkinson's three greatest teams at Oklahoma were those of 1949, 1955, and 1956. The 1949 team had great depth, alternating two lines for half of each quarter, each playing offense and defense. The offensive backs, Darrell Royal, Lindell Pearson, George Thomas (the nation's scoring leader that year), and Heath gave way to four defensive backs who also were good enough to spell them as a unit on offense. That season, Oklahoma scored 364 points and was Number 1 in rushing offense; allowed only 88 points and was Number 1 in rushing defense; won all ten games; and crushed LSU 35-0 in the Sugar Bowl. Wilkinson was chosen Coach of the Year for the only time at Oklahoma, though his team the following year with another 10-0 record, won its first national title in what may have been his best coaching job, because Heath was the only returning starter. Wilkinson said that team "possessed as much heart as I have ever seen," noting it came from behind to win three times in the fourth quarter.

While Wilkinson always considered his fourth-ranked 1952 team, led by Heisman Trophy winner Vessels and which averaged more than 40 points a game with an 8-1-1 record, stronger than the 1950 national champions, there were no doubts about the 1955 and 1956 teams. Halfback Tommy McDonald blazed a path for those teams, which were renowned both for their speed and their defense. In 1955, the Sooners scored 365 points and allowed just 54, shut out their last four opponents, and for the second time in three years, beat Maryland in the Orange Bowl. The first time, in 1953, the undefeated Terps were crowned national champions (there was no post-season polling at that time) and Wilkinson's fourth-ranked Sooners spoiled their season with a gutsy 7-0 victory, twice stopping Maryland inside the 10-yard line in the first half. Larry Grigg's 25-yard TD run capped an 80-yard, second period drive for Oklahoma's only score.

The 1956 team, with Clendon Thomas' inside running providing a perfect partner to McDonald's outside speed, probably was Wilkinson's best because it averaged more than 46 points a game and never scored fewer than 27; it shut out five of its 10 opponents; and it was crowned national champion in a landslide vote. Its record-setting winning streak continued in 1957 until the Sooners met Notre Dame in Norman, Oklahoma in early November. The Irish, thrashed 40-0 the previous year, shut down Oklahoma's offense and upset the Sooners 7-0 on Dick Lynch's short third-quarter sweep.

It was Wilkinson's first defeat in 47 games, and only the ninth since he became the Sooners' coach 11 seasons earlier. No coach since has ever come close to matching such excellence, which is why he is in the elite group of coaches who have been inducted into the Hall of Fame and received the Amos Alonzo Stagg Award, coaching's greatest honor.

Left: *Clendon Thomas led the nation in scoring in 1956 and was the main weapon in Wilkinson's national championship team that was in the midst of a record-setting 47-game winning streak.*

FIELDING YOST

Record:

Ohio Wesleyan (1897)	7-1-1
Nebraska (1898)	7-4-0
Kansas (1899)	10-0-0
Stanford (1900)	7-2-1
Michigan (1901-23)	151-27-10
(1925-26)	14-2-0

Below: *Fielding H. Yost inherited a bankrupt athletic department at the University of Michigan in 1901 and brought it to a peak of excellence that it still enjoys nearly a century later.*

"Hurry up! Hurry up! Hurry up!"

For a quarter-century, that cry reverberated through the Michigan football practice field every day, and became so much a part of the daily routine that it was only natural that its originator, Fielding Harris Yost, would forever be better known as "Hurry Up" Yost.

From the moment he stepped off a train from Palo Alto, California, after a year of coaching Stanford, Yost was dedicated to the personal mission of establishing Michigan as the premier football power in the country, and himself as the pre-eminent coach. Four of his first five teams – the "point-a-minute" Wolverines – won or shared the Western Conference (now Big Ten) championship and scored over 2800 points to just 42 by their opponents (in only 57 games!) They played 54 consecutive games without a loss. Two of his last four teams also were unbeaten, and won or shared conference titles.

In between, Yost co-existed on equal terms, though not in his own mind, with such coaching legends as Knute Rockne, Bob Zuppke, Dr. Harry Williams, Amos Alonzo Stagg and Pop Warner as a prime contributor to the development of the modern game of football. Unlike Warner or Stagg, he was not a voracious innovator, but if anyone was looking for a good, rock-solid philosophy by which to build a winner, then Yost was the man. His teams were well-balanced on offense and defense, never flashy or physically superior, but always smarter and better drilled in fundamentals than the opposition. He developed the "Yost System," which some called "punt, pass and prayer." It was percentage football, because a Yost-coached team never wasted energy by pounding an opponent in

Above left: *Germany Schultz is considered one of the greatest centers ever to play for Michigan. He was a member of Yost's great "point-a-minute" teams.*

Far left and left: *Neil Snow teamed with Willie Heston (left) to give Yost a great backfield duo for his "point-a-minute" teams. Heston was a world class sprinter and a halfback, while Snow was a fine inside runner, the perfect backfield force.*

Michigan territory. It always punted on first or second down and allowed the opposition to wear itself out trying to cover big amounts of territory. All the while, Michigan waited to capitalize on and score on an opponent's mistake in its territory.

In his final game as a head coach, against Minnesota, the Wolverines had a net rushing gain of 25 yards compared to the Gophers' 400, but still won the game 7-6. Time and again, Minnesota drove down the field, was stopped by Michigan's defense, and then Yost had his team immediately kick the ball back – and the sequence was repeated. Finally, Michigan end Bennie Oosterbaan picked up a fumble at midfield and ran for a touchdown, and Benny Friedman kicked the winning point.

"Every so-called system is 95 percent fundamentals," Yost said. "You must have the proper blocking, charging and tackling if you're going to have a system. You also must have the proper cogs to fit the machine to make it work."

Yost had the cogs, and his "machine" was the most awesome team in the early part of this century, with such players as Willie Heston, Neil Snow, Germany Schultz, Dan McGugin and Boss Weekes. He built a team from the center out, and the six-foot, four-inch, 240-pound Schultz was one of the greatest ever to play the position. He wanted balance in his backfield – speed to the outside, power to the inside – and found it in Heston and Snow. Heston could beat world class sprinters over the first 40 yards, which reflects a back's essential ingredient – quickness. Snow was a powerful fullback, giving his run offense perfect balance.

Even though critics lamented his "punt, pass and pray" style, Yost's teams never were dull nor lacking imagination when they unleashed their power. They weren't easy to play, either. Illinois coach Bob Zuppke said Yost's teams "knock you down, and run away from you, but when you try the same thing on them, they knock you down again." Yost once had tried unsuccessfully to ban the forward pass, then found it a great weapon as early as 1907. His 1925 team, which he called his best, had a great passing attack with Friedman and Oosterbaan, the famed "Benny-to-Bennie" combination. He claimed that the Wolverines had only one pass intercepted during his coaching tenure at Ann Arbor.

Yost also had an arsenal of seven plays which he used when his teams were in scoring position, the most deadly being "Old 83," which scored hundreds of touchdowns. It was a quarterback-keeper

Left: *Yost's great "point-a-minute" teams scored more than 2800 points in just 57 games. He also won Big Ten titles with two of his last four Michigan teams in the 1920s, which he considered even better than his early juggernauts.*

that developed off a pair of fakes to backs heading in opposite directions, with the quarterback keeping the ball and running to the short side after the defensive end chased the second fake. He also claimed to be the first to name and number plays.

But his rapid-fire offense gave added impetus to his "Hurry Up" reputation. The quarterback began calling the next play as soon as the runner was tackled as players jumped into their positions. The next number he called was the starting signal, and the center instantly snapped the ball. The play leaped into motion, often catching the opposition either flat-footed or offsides.

Yost never stopped coaching, even when he wasn't on the practice field. He would meet a player on campus, stop and soon begin demonstrating a technique. When his team was quartered at a Minneapolis hotel, a stranger in the lobby

asked him about a play. Yost grabbed everyone within reach, lined them up in formation and still needed two bodies. So he grabbed a bellhop carrying some bags, and used him and one of the bags to fill out the formation. The lady to whom the bag belonged was irate. "This is disgraceful!" she shrieked. "Where is the manager?"

"Hold your horses just a minute," Yost said. "The manager is playing quarterback."

Yost was a physically vigorous man, having been a teenage marshall in the rough-and-tumble hills of West Virginia. He played football for Lafayette and West Virginia, and in the town teams that spawned professional football. He started coaching in 1897 at Ohio Wesleyan, and his team beat Ohio State and tied Michigan. Yost spent a year at Nebraska, had an undefeated team and Missouri Valley Conference champion at Kansas, then headed west in

Above: *Michigan boosters honored Yost with a brand new car before his final game as head coach, and as athletic director he honored them by building 106,000-seat Michigan Stadium which Wolverine teams still fill every game.*

Right: *Yost also turned out successful men from his teams. Here he is pictured with three former players who became members of Congress, from left: Rep. Frank James, Yost, Sen. Arthur Vandenberg and Rep. Robert H. Chaney.*

Opposite: *Yost was not above a little horseplay now and then as he poses in full equipment with the star of his 1926 team, Benny Friedman (right). Friedman was one of the greatest passers in the school's history, and teamed with future Wolverine coach Bennie Oosterbaan for the famous "Benny-to-Bennie" passing attack.*

1900 to Stanford, where he won the Pacific Coast championship. That year he also coached four other teams to championships, including San Jose Teacher's College where he discovered Heston, and brought him to Michigan the following year when the Pacific Coast Conference forbade schools to hire non-alumni as coaches.

Michigan's athletic program was impoverished when Yost arrived, and less than two dozen prospects from a student body of 2000 turned out for football. Yet, in his first season, the Wolverines "hurry-upped" themselves to 10 victories without a loss, and scored 550 points without allowing any! At the end of the season, the Tournament of Roses Committee, looking to highlight their New Year's Day celebration, invited Michigan to play Stanford. Never one to forget a slight, real or imagined, Yost turned down his hosts' request for 35-minute halves, and used just 11 players to build a 37-0 lead. Stanford coach C. M. Fickert wanted to end the game, saying his players were exhausted.

"Rest 'em," Yost told Fickert, "then put them back in."

When the score reached 49-0, Stanford's players just walked off the field.

From that season on, Michigan's athletic program rode a tidal wave of success, first on the crest of Yost's coaching, and then under his leadership as athletic director that ultimately resulted in a $3-million complex when he retired in 1941. Yost retired as coach after 1923, but had second thoughts when Zuppke's Illinois team, featuring Red Grange, wrecked the Wolverines in 1924. Zuppke presided at a coaches' committee meeting in New York after the season, and refused to recognize a resolution offered by Yost, noting, "The man addressing the chair is an athletic director, not a football coach, and athletic directors are not eligible for membership. This man ceased being a football coach one sunny afternoon last October at Champaign."

Yost was insulted. Zuppke tried to pacify him by saying he was only joking. But Yost brushed him off: "I'm going to be a football coach next season, Zuppke, and what's more, I promise you that I'll beat you."

Yost returned for two more seasons, and Michigan beat the Illini 3-0 on Friedman's field goal. Yost's defense held Grange to just one yard.

The "Yost System" always prevailed.

BOB ZUPPKE

Record:

Illinois (1913-41) 131-81-13

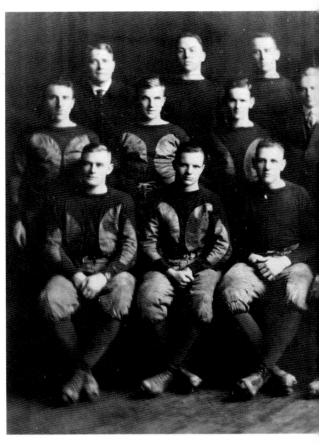

"Zup had more color than two rainbows."

That was how famed sports columnist Grantland Rice once described Bob Zuppke, who coached at Illinois for 29 seasons, the second longest continuous tenure by any coach in Big Ten history (tied by Ohio State's Woody Hayes) to Amos Alonzo Stagg.

In terms of common perception of what a football coach is supposed to be, Zuppke probably was an exception to every rule ever made. He was an artist whose work hung in galleries, he could match quips with the best, and he was a master innovator whose fertile mind produced such now-common features as the screen pass, the huddle, the flea flicker pass, the spiral pass from center, guards dropping back to help protect the passer as well as dropping them off the line of scrimmage to a new position called "linebacker."

Below: Bob Zuppke was one of the few coaches in college football history to move directly from high school into a head coaching job at a major university.

He was the consummate believer in amateurism, and never had a scholarship player during all of his years at Illinois. "The honor of playing for Illinois is payment enough," he said, and while it often left him at a competitive disadvantage, he never budged from that belief.

Zuppke was a robust little coach, who was born in Berlin, Germany in 1872, and moved to Milwaukee with his parents two years later. He never lost his German accent, which became heavier when he got excited, and he often clipped off his words and his sentences as he steamed along. He taught school for a year after attending a teacher's normal school, and then enrolled at the University of Wisconsin. He was a quarterback on the freshman team, but his size was an impediment to varsity play. However, he played basketball and was a member of the Badgers' 1902 championship team.

Since he didn't play much, he absorbed everything possible from the coaches and schooled himself in basic football. Yet, it was a love of painting – he once dropped out of high school for a year to paint signs – that drove him to New York where he worked for illustrators for a year. He returned to the Midwest and got a job in a Grand Rapids, Michigan advertising agency until the owners discovered him running a sports club within the offices, complete with scheduled boxing matches.

While Zuppke was in the East, he went to Yale University and talked his way into practice – a no-no for a non-Yale graduate – where he accumulated more football knowledge. Torn between

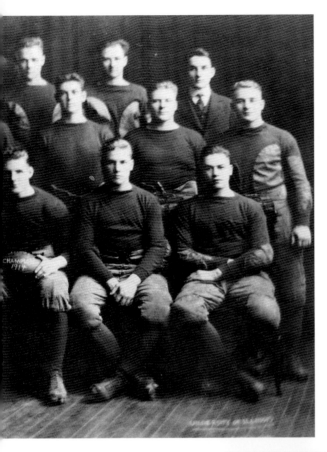

his love of art and the sport of football, he finally gave the latter his attention the day he was fired from the ad agency. He learned of a high school coaching vacancy in Muskegon, Michigan and got the job for $1000 a year. He won the state prep title his first year, and six years later was paid $2000 to coach Oak Park High School, in Illinois, where his teams gained a national reputation. He lost his first two games and never lost again during his three years at the school. His team travelled from coast-to-coast and beat every highly-rated high school team.

It was during his high school coaching days that Zuppke's innovations gained life. At Oak Park, he came up with the "flea flicker" pass, his version using a pass to an end who then "flicked" a lateral to a trailing halfback running at full speed. It was his favorite play, and he used it in 1925 when his Illini team, featuring Red Grange, stunned Penn on muddy Franklin Field. He used that one off a fake field goal.

At Oak Park, he also came up with his "Flying Trapeze" play, calling for three laterals and a forward pass. This play stunned unbeaten Ohio State in 1934, the only loss the Buckeyes suffered that year, and it cost them the Big Ten and national

Above: Zuppke's 1914 team at Illinois produced a perfect 7-0 record and the first of back-to-back Big Ten championships. Zuppke won or shared six conference championships at Illinois.

Right: Zuppke (right) and his coaching staff at Illinois, where he always seemed to produce a big upset each season. His biggest may have occurred in 1916 when Illinois, a five-touchdown underdog, defeated Minnesota.

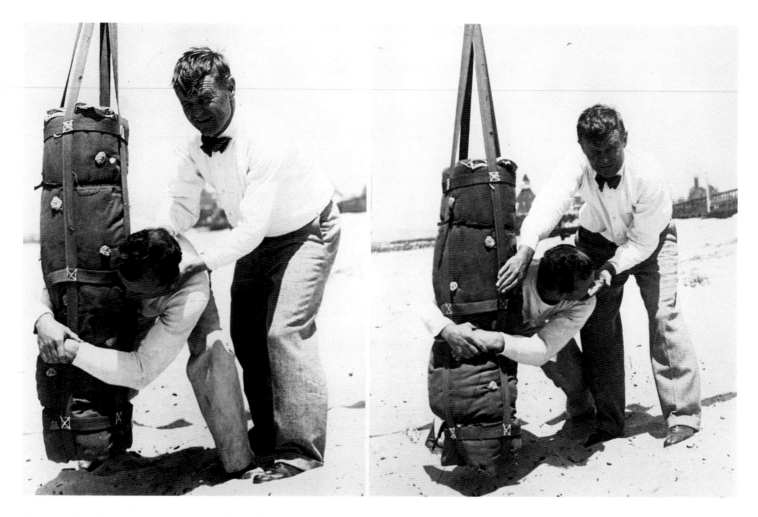

Above: *Zuppke was a meticulous teacher, and his ability to prepare his teams thoroughly for a game often compensated for a lack of top-flight talent, earning him the nickname "Master of the Upset."*

championships. He trained his center at Muskegon to spiral a ball between his legs to a kicker, and it took another 10 years before that style was accepted at college level.

With his Oak Park team so powerful and successful, it was a natural move for the University of Illinois to hire him, but only after Zuppke had considered offers for more money from several other schools. He signed for $2750 a year "because I had better material at Illinois."

That was probably the only time in his career he ever said that, because the Illini, under Zuppke, always were undermanned. He preferred light, speedy players, and his heaviest team averaged only 182 pounds. Mostly, they were in the high 160s.

He made up for this lack with his coaching. Zuppke combined meticulous preparation, some farsighted thinking and his ever-present sense of humor to keep his team playing at a level that often exceeded its talent. In so doing, he became known as the "master of the upset," and that reputation was a pair of bookends which spanned his career.

The first occurred in 1916, when Illinois was a five-touchdown underdog against Minnesota. The Gophers had outscored three previous opponents 198-0, but the wily Zuppke wasn't awed. He scrimmaged his own team five times before the game, noting: "We're supposed to get killed Saturday, so

at least we'll have the pleasure of doing it ourselves."

When his team had its final practice at Minnesota's stadium, it was so tight that it looked inept. Zuppke called a halt, and told his players to take the night off: "Eat, drink and be merry, you have nothing to lose." He even took them to a show, and got them back to their hotel past midnight. The next day, before going onto the field, he said that Minnesota would run three specific plays, and if they stopped them, they could win.

That is exactly what happened. Illinois got the ball after a wobbly punt, and scored as Zuppke unveiled a new spread formation that totally confounded the Gophers. Illinois took a 14-0 lead at the half and held on to win 14-9, a game considered one of the greatest upsets ever in college football.

When he was just two years from retirement, mighty Michigan, with its All-America back Tom Harmon, was a huge favorite over an Illinois team that had scored just one touchdown in four games. Illinois won 16-7, and the game was noted as the upset of the year.

In between those momentous games, Zuppke's teams were renowned as spoilers. In 1921, the Illini had lost all four conference games, and in the season's final game, upset unbeaten Ohio State in Columbus to kill the Bucks' title hopes. In 1922, they did the same thing to Wisconsin.

Of course, Zuppke also coached Red Grange, one of college football's greatest stars. Zuppke always insisted that he was the greatest runner in the history of the game, and his evidence is strong to support that belief. In 1924, Grange rode rough-shod over Michigan as the Illini trounced the Wolverines 39-14. That same year, Illinois went east to play Penn, and on a muddy field, Grange scored four times in the first quarter.

There were no coaching secrets here. "We played the law of averages with Red," Zuppke said. "He was a great runner, so we made sure he had plenty of opportunities to use his talents. I had a standing order with Harry Hall, my quarterback, to give the ball to Red 30 times a game. With that many carries, he was almost certain to get away several times for long runs."

Ironically, the Grange-era teams were not Zuppke's best. "They were weak defensively," Zuppke said. But none outranked his 1927-29 teams – "the average man's team," he called them,

Right: *Red Grange and Zuppke, who brought Illinois some of its greatest football moments in the mid-1920s.*

Below: *Zuppke started an all-sophomore team in his final season, 1942, because wartime constraints had stripped him of all upperclassmen.*

because there were no great stars. Illinois lost only two games in those three seasons, won a pair of Big Ten titles and finished second a third time.

Zuppke was as colorful a coach as he was talented. He was renowned for his endless list of slogans: "Often an All-America is made by a long run, a weak defense and a poet in the press box;" "Good losers, I don't like 'em. Show me a team of singers in defeat. I want bad losers." One day he exhorted his team "not to come off the field alive" against Iowa. When he dispatched a substitute for an injured player, he was startled to see the young man back at the bench.

"What are you doing back here?" Zuppke asked.

"Coach, the guy's still breathing," the player replied.

While presiding at the American Football Coaches Association meeting, he endured an impassioned speech in nomination of a midwestern coach for the top job, and then nominated himself, pointedly telling the southern members, "Do you want some Yankee ruling your group? Didn't you have enough of that?" The final vote was 499 to 1 –

and Zuppke, true to his often zany ways, had voted for the other guy.

His last great teams were led by Pack Benyon, a fine passer. They lost the Big Ten titles in 1933 and 1934 by a total of six points. Those teams averaged about 170 pounds per man, and as he usually did, Zuppke converted halfbacks into fullbacks, and depended on clever execution on the field, and his coaching, for success. From that point, until he retired in 1941, the glory days were past. He survived a vote by the school's athletic board to oust him in 1938 because the board of trustees came to his defense.

His next to final game was a 21-0 loss to Ohio State, and Buckeyes coach Paul Brown recalls meeting Zuppke in the center of the field after the game and him saying: "Some days, you got the boys, you beat old Zup. Some days, Zup got the boys and he beat you."

"And with that," Brown noted, "he was gone. I had never met him before, and that was all he said."

But for four decades, his teams and his contributions had spoken mightily. And they still do.

Above: *Red Grange stunned Michigan in 1924, scoring four touchdowns, three in the first 12 minutes of the game. Here he runs for his final TD in a 39-14 victory.*

Opposite: *Grange and his famed Number 77 jersey. His "Galloping Ghost" nickname was well-earned, because he set an all-time collegiate rushing mark during his three seasons at Illinois under Zuppke.*

INDEX

Numbers in *italics* indicate illustrations